AMERICAN VISIONARY FICTION

Kennikat Press
National University Publications
Literary Criticism Series

General Editor
John E. Becker
Fairleigh Dickinson University

RICHARD FINHOLT

AMERICAN VISIONARY FICTION

Mad Metaphysics as Salvation Psychology

National University Publications
KENNIKAT PRESS // 1978
Port Washington, N. Y. // London

Manufactured in the United States of America

Published by
Kennikat Press Corp.
Port Washington, N. Y. / London

Library of Congress Cataloging in Publication Data

Finholt, Richard.
  American visionary fiction

  (Literary criticism series) (National university publications)
    Bibliography: p.
    Includes index.
    1. American fiction—History and criticism.
I. Title.
PS371.F56   813'.009   77-5346
ISBN 0-8046-9191-6

For Mary Kay

ACKNOWLEDGMENTS

I would like to give special thanks to Professor James Mellard of Northern Illinois University without whose friendship and counsel I could never have undertaken this study. I would also like to give special thanks to Professor Julian Markels of Ohio State University who gave me his total support at the time when it was most needed. Chapter Six originally appeared in a somewhat different form in the *Georgia Review*. Chapter Eight originally appeared in a somewhat different form in *Modern Fiction Studies*. I am grateful to the editors of those publications.

CONTENTS

AMERICAN VISIONARY FICTION

As I was watching, there was a Watcher,
a Holy One coming down from heaven.
He cried aloud and said,
"Hew down the tree, lop off the branches,
strip away the foliage, scatter the fruit.
   Let the wild beasts flee from its shelter
      and the birds from its branches,
but leave the stump with its roots in the ground.
   So, tethered with an iron ring,
   let him eat his fill of the lush grass;
   let him be drenched with the dew of heaven
   and share the lot of the beasts in their pasture;
   let his mind cease to be a man's mind,
   and let him be given the mind of a beast.
   Let seven times pass over him.
   The issue has been determined by the Watchers
   and the sentence pronounced by the Holy Ones.

                    Daniel 4:13–17, [*New English Bible*]

He saw God's foot upon the treadle of the loom,
and spoke it; and therefore his shipmates called
him mad. So man's insanity is heaven's sense; and
wandering from all mortal reason, man comes at last
to that celestial thought, which, to reason, is
absurd and frantic; and weal or woe, feels then
uncompromised, indifferent as his God.

                    Chapter 93, "The Castaway," *Moby-Dick*

PART ONE

THE MURDER OF MOBY DICK

1

THE SUBTERRANEAN MINER

There are two sorts of writers. Or so says Norman Mailer in *Cannibals and Christians*. With the first, the tone of his work belongs "to the subject more than to the author—professional football is seen as professional football and ladies' fashion as ladies' fashion." The second kind of writer, says Mailer, "can be better or worse, but the writings always have a touch of the grandiose, even the megalomaniacal: the reason may be that the writings are part of a continuing and more or less comprehensive vision of existence into which everything must fit." To the empirically minded, this may seem like putting the cart before the horse, but the assumption is that what would be self-delusion to the first kind of writer is the way to deepest hidden truth for the second. Mailer continues: "The unspoken urge is to find secret relations between professional football and ladies' fashion and bring them in alive as partners to the vision."

I propose to study some writers in America who seem to fit into Mailer's second category. Edgar Allan Poe and Herman Melville in the last century; Norman Mailer and Ralph Ellison and James Dickey in this century.

The way to truth for the first kind of writer is through a study of "men in the world." Tolstoy worked this way, according to Mailer, while Dostoevsky, representative of the second group, chose to tell the stories of isolated individuals "illuminated by the terror of exploring the mysteries of themselves." Mailer describes *An American Tragedy* as a product of the first kind of writer and *Moby-Dick* as a product of the second ("the voyage of Ahab into his obsession"), and, he concludes: "The serious novel begins from a fixed philosophical point—the desire to discover reality—and it goes to search for that reality in society, or else must embark on a trip up the upper Amazon of the inner eye."

The voyage into the darkest regions of the inner eye has been the great theme of some of our most important fiction writers, a point nicely made by Harry Levin in *The Power of Blackness* and Richard Chase in *The American Novel and Its Tradition*. But both critics seem to have avoided certain implications of the romantic fascination of American writers with the *self*. What have they found there that has led them away from social values to the condition of, in Chase's words, "alienation, contradiction, and disorder?" In Levin's words: "In response to the widespread notion of American gregariousness, they would urge the counterclaims of individualism, not infrequently carried to the point of isolation and alienation."

Levin, I believe, suggests the wrong answer when he keys on the following passage from Melville's "Hawthorne and His Mosses": ". . . this great power of blackness in him derives its force from its appeal to that Calvinistic sense of Innate Depravity and Original Sin, from whose visitations, in some shape or other, no deeply thinking mind is always and wholly free." From this Levin concludes: "Applying the touchstone of Shakespeare's tragedies to Hawthorne's tales, the crucial trait that fixed and fascinated Melville was what he designated 'the power of blackness.'" But the gist of Melville's article makes clear that the trait that "fixed and fascinated" him was, instead, "the deeply thinking mind." Levin should have paid more attention to the following passage and then called his book *The Madness of Vital Truth:*

But it is those deep far-away things in him [Shakespeare] ; those occasional flashings-forth of the intuitive Truth in him; those short, quick probings at the very axis of reality;—these are the things that make Shakespeare, Shakespeare. Through the mouths of the dark characters of Hamlet,

Timon, Lear, and Iago, he craftily says, or sometimes insinuates the things which we feel to be so terrifically true, that it were all but madness for any good man, in his own proper character, to utter, or even hint of them. Tormented into desperation, Lear, the frantic king, tears off the mask, and speaks the same madness of vital truth.

Melville calls the crucial trait the "great, deep intellect," and he divides the world of writers into those who have it and those who do not. All writers, he implies, write from a certain fund of "humor and love" but those that we call "genius" have the "great, deep intellect" as "the indispensable complement of these." Melville would not have known what Chase is talking about when he describes the "scrupulous art-consciousness" that supposedly motivated an American writer like Hawthorne, because, for Melville, the "great beauty in such a mind [as Hawthorne's] is but the product of its strength." I would like to superimpose Melville's binary classification system on Mailer's and suggest that Melville's pronouncement represents the beginnings of an *intellectual* tradition in American fiction, a tradition that takes the inner self as subject because the deeply thinking mind is naturally drawn to its mysteries and the vision that arises from them and not because of some Byronic fascination with morbid emotions.

Levin's orientation makes more of the blackness phrase than seems to have been intended. There is nothing about being gloomy that gives a writer the power to say the "terrifically true." To think so would be to put the effect before the cause. It is simply Melville's conviction that the truth to be found beneath the individual's social "mask" is such that any man courageous enough to let his mind probe beneath it will be led to say the kind of black, disorienting things that will lead those still in their socially "proper" characters to call that man mad. Melville's is a romantic tradition which rejects the too-easy assumptions of English romanticism because it has been bred within the confines of Calvinistic, Puritan logic. Melville's apostrophe to Bulkington in *Moby-Dick,* while maintaining the romantic and un-Puritan ideal of unlimited aspiration, does not celebrate the questing imagination, does not celebrate the "spontaneous overflow of powerful feelings," but, rather, the courageous effort of the rational mind to keep questing on a sea whose storm warnings spell either madness or the death of the intellect:

Know ye, now, Bulkington? Glimpses do ye seem to see of that mortally intolerable truth; that all *deep, earnest thinking* is but the intrepid effort of the soul to keep the open independence of her sea; while the wildest winds of heaven and earth conspire to cast her on the treacherous, slavish shore? [my italics]

However the winds of heaven might blow, the winds of earth blow wild indeed. Melville's critical reputation was swept away, Perry Miller tells us in *The Raven and the Whale,* by a cultural hurricane of confused and conflicting values which Melville never completely understood. But if Mailer's critical reputation is in constant danger it is because he understands his society's pretensions and confusions only too well; he begs that society in the epigraph to *The Deer Park,* "Please do not understand me too quickly." Mailer's manifesto of undying antagonism to a society too dense to appreciate the wonderful mystery of his own powerful mind appears in Sergius's musings at the conclusion of the novel:

For do we not gamble our way to the heart of the mystery against all the power of good manners, good morals, the fear of germs, and the sense of sin? Not to mention the prisons of pain, the wading pools of pleasure, and the public professional voices of our sentimental land. If there is a God, and sometimes I believe there is one, I'm sure He says, "Go on, my boy. I don't know that I can help you, but we wouldn't want all *those* people to tell you what to do."

Mailer understands, as no American writer since Melville, that "man's insanity is heaven's sense," that such a notion threatens the Mosaic foundations of our society, and that the writer seeking a vision of heaven's sense can expect to be declared as mad as his fictional characters by a society secure in its belief that its highest values reflect those of heaven. If Melville read carefully the following passage from *The Scarlet Letter,* he had a pretty good idea why Hawthorne never answered his effusive letter in praise of *The House of Seven Gables:*

. . . the sufferer's conscience [Chillingworth's] had been kept in an irritated state, the tendency of which was, not to cure by wholesome pain, but to disorganize and corrupt his spiritual being. Its result, on earth, could hardly fail to be insanity, and hereafter, that eternal alienation from the Good and True, of which madness is perhaps the earthly type.

Melville's *Moby-Dick* was attacked most viciously by the organs of the Democratic Party of his day, according to Miller, because they felt some of Melville's intellectual "self-esteem" a threat to democratic and nationalistic ideals. And Mailer and James Dickey were the recent victims of a remarkably moralistic, double-barreled attack in the November 1972 issue of *College English*. Frederic Jameson mounted a nicely modulated Marxist critique that concluded that Dickey was to be despised for his "machismo" and Mailer rather to be pitied for absorbing a little more of capitalism's decadence than his delicate psyche can bear. But Sol Yurick attacks Jameson in a following comment for not going far enough in his condemnation of these two perpetrators of a "counterrevolutionary tradition." The "isolate agonist" that each conceives as his fictional hero, says Yurick, not only reflects its "writer" but the decadent system, "Capitalism," which "emerges" both; whatever higher truth Dickey and Mailer might think they are serving, Yurick implies, there can be no truth "more primal" than the class warfare which each unwittingly perpetuates. And Jameson, in his turn, is not ashamed to admit, "I am defending something a little more complicated than the proposition that bad politics mades bad literature." A little, but not much. One would have thought that the New Critics and the Structuralists had killed this kind of systematic confusion of the work with the author's imagined intentions, or at least had driven it underground, but the image of the "isolate agonist" (a nice phrase for the heroes created by these writers) is so threatening to establishment ideals that the author of such heresy must be attacked.

Mailer thrives on such attacks, because, after all, if one is being criticized by *those* people, one must be getting close to "mortally intolerable truth." Mailer reports on a classic Mailer confrontation early in *The Armies of the Night*. His antagonist is leftist intellectual Paul Goodman, who had attacked Mailer in the pages of *Dissent* as "the false prophet of orgasm" who "was naturally attracted to the false hero of Washington [Kennedy] who went in for wargasms." This is obviously the kind of childish, word-game cheap-shot that was to earn Gore Vidal a head butt from Mailer after he mindlessly compared Mailer to Charles Manson. But Mailer does not waste the pages of his only prize-winning book on a cheap-shot; he is aiming at the root confusions in Goodman's thinking. Goodman could not seem on surer ground than in advocating a rational acceptance of sex as a natural human activity and not something dirty or shameful, but then comes Mailer sailing the disturbingly open freedom of his storm-tossed sea:

His [Mailer's] fundamental animus to Goodman was still, unhappily, on sex. Goodman's ideas tended to declare in rough that heterosexuality, homosexuality, and onanism were equal valid forms of activity, best denuded of guilt. Mailer, with his neo-Victorianism, thought that if there was anything worse than homosexuality and masturbation, it was putting the two together. The super-hygiene of all this mental prophylaxis offended him profoundly. Super-hygiene impregnated the air with medicated Vaseline—there was nothing dirty in the stuff; and sex to Mailer's idea of it was better off dirty, damned, even slavish! than clean and without guilt.

Some critics, ready to understand Mailer as quickly as possible for the good of the society, never get beyond thinking of Mailer as the crazed defender of dirty sex for guilt's sake. But some read on to discover in the very next lines the rationale for this statement in Mailer's conviction that society is the arch-enemy of the primal truths hidden at the bottom of the self:

For guilt was the existential edge of sex. Without guilt, sex was meaningless. One advanced into sex against one's sense of guilt, and each time guilt was successfully defied, one had learned a little more about the contractual relation of one's own existence to the unheard thunders of the deep—each time guilt herded one back with authority, some primitive awe—hence some creative clue to the rages of the deep—was left to brood about. Onanism and homosexuality were not, to Mailer, light vices—to him it sometimes seemed that much of life and most of society were designed precisely to drive men deep into onanism and homosexuality; one defied such a fate by sweeping up the psychic profit which derived from the existential assertion of yourself—which was a way of saying that nobody was born a man; you earned manhood provided you were good enough, bold enough.

For those ready to agree by now that Mailer's inner voices are indeed grandiose and megalomaniacal if nothing else, I remind them that nothing is sacred to his probing intellect, not even, as some would charge, his own ego. When he, as the hero of one of his new-journalistic pieces (Mailer has long since dropped the pretense that he has ever been able to find or create an intellect more interesting than his own and therefore capable of being a hero he can take seriously), has not been "good enough, bold enough," he is his own harshest critic, as in his entertaining account in *The Presidential Papers* of a battle of verbal wit with former heavyweight champion Charles "Sonny" Liston, a battle which Mailer loses:

Now it came over me that I had not begun to have the strength this morning to be so very good as I had wanted to be. Once more I had tried to become a hero, and had ended as an eccentric. There would be argument later whether I was a monster or a clown. Could it be, was I indeed a bum?

And it is with such a fragile "ego" that writers like Melville and Mailer are prepared to abandon the orderliness of culture to create inner voyages to eternity, the ego nothing but a "carpet-bag," as Melville wrote to Hawthorne on 16 April 1851, when all of society, "those *yes*-gentry, they travel with heaps of baggage, and, damn them! they will never get through the Custom House." The "NO! in thunder" is to society and not to God or nature. The central fact about all these writers, one that critics like Jameson and Yurick cannot accept, is that they have dedicated their work to what they consider a higher order than that of society, and a man cannot serve two masters. It is not that they do not believe in "the Good and True"; they just do not believe that it can be found through the auspices of social values. To say NO to society, then, is to say YES to the vision within.

In defining the dynamics of these distinctly American literary visions, Chase has been helpful, but he clearly does not arrive at an analysis of the crucial factor that makes American writers say NO so thunderously:

The English novel, one might say, has been a kind of imperial enterprise, an appropriation of reality with the high purpose of bringing order to disorder. By contrast, as Lawrence observed . . . the American novel has usually seemed content to explore, rather than to appropriate and civilize, the remarkable and in some ways unexampled territories of life in the New World and to reflect its anomalies and dilemmas. It has not wanted to build an imperium but merely to discover a new place and a new state of mind. Explorers see more deeply, darkly, privately and disinterestedly than imperialists, who must perforce be circumspect and prudential. The American novel is more profound and clairvoyant than the English novel, but by the same token it is narrower and more arbitrary, and it tends to carve out of experience brilliant, highly wrought fragments rather than massive unities.

If the works of the five writers studied here are "clairvoyant," however, it is precisely because the visions they carve out of private, fragmented experience are of "massive unities," though not of unities born of the social contract but of "the contractual relation of one's own existence to the unheard thunders of the deep."

The "great, deep intellect" is obsessed with its vision of the whole and will settle for nothing less. For this reason Melville in his poem "The Aeolian Harp" satirized one of Emerson's favorite symbols; he recognized that Emerson's basic cognitive principle ("every natural fact is a symbol of some spiritual fact") somehow fails in apprehending the reality of chaos and evil in the universe. For this reason alone Melville is excited to find that Hawthorne's thinking, contrary to much of the socially acceptable thinking of the day, makes allowance for the metaphysical implications of the physical existence of evil: "No man can weigh this world without throwing in something, somehow like Original Sin, to strike the uneven balance." And if Melville seems more interested in disrupting accepted beliefs, in disorientation, in alienation from the culture of his day, this is only because, as Newton Arvin makes clear in his critical biography *Herman Melville,* he saw the necessity of shedding inadequate systems before one can arrive at an all-embracing "myth" of one's own:

He was unique . . . among American writers of his time in the particular quality of his intellectual and moral seriousness; unique in his troubled preoccupations with problems that Emerson and Thoreau simply passed by, and that Hawthorne was intellectually too incurious to consider deeply. Like a truly myth-making poet's, Melville's imagination was obsessed by the spectacle of a natural and human scene in which the instinctive need for order and meaning seems mainly to be confronted by meaninglessness and disorder; in which the human will seems some-times to be sustained but oftener to be thwarted by the forces of physical nature, and even by agencies that lie behind it; in which goodness and evil, beneficence and destructiveness, light and darkness, seem bafflingly intermixed. In none of the great formulations that were available to him, neither in Calvinist Christianity nor in romantic optimism, could Melville discover a myth that for him was adequate to the lighting up of these obscurities.

And the same restlessness with easily assimilated forms, the same plunging into "obscurities," is exactly what the sympathetic reader finds in Norman Mailer's work, according to Richard Poirier in his critical study *Norman Mailer:*

I suspect that an enthusiasm for his work means that one shares his partiality for those moments where more is happening than one can very easily assimilate. By and large, the other contemporary writers I have mentioned [Updike, Roth, and Malamud; the same writers Mailer would put in his first, "men in the world" category] will not allow more to happen than can be accounted for in the forms they have settled upon. They work away from rather than into the ultimate inconsistencies, the central incoherence in the way we live now. Mailer, on the other hand, is always looking for the stylistic equivalent for that movement of "the ego in perpetual transit from tower to dungeon and back again."

What unites Melville and Mailer, and them with the other writers studied here, finally, is a modernistic conviction that unconscious urges at the source of the inner Amazon are the keys to deciphering the whole. Melville's metaphor of "the subterranean miner," for example, conveys brilliantly the "collective" nature of the unconscious that Freud and Jung would later postulate. Ishmael is grasping to explain what Mailer would call the "secret relations" between Ahab's madness and his crew's spontaneous willingness to be mad with him, and Ishmael wonders:

How was it that they so aboundingly responded to the old man's ire—by what evil magic their souls were possessed, that at times his hate seemed almost theirs; the White Whale as much their insufferable foe as his; how all this came to be—what the White Whale was to them, or how to their *unconscious* understandings, also, in some dim, unsuspected way, he might have seemed the gliding great demon of the seas of life,—all this to explain would be to dive deeper than Ishmael can go. The subterranean miner that works in us all, how can one tell whither leads his shaft by the ever shifting, muffled sound of his pick? [my italics]

And one hundred and more years later Mailer's fictional themes are a continuation of the attempt to map the movements of the unseen miner, a job, he says in *Cannibals and Christians,* he is hesitant to leave to such admittedly brilliant modern philosophers as Sartre and Heidegger: ". . . I suspect they are no closer to the buried continent of existentialism than were medieval cartographers near to a useful map of the world. The new continent which shows on our psychic maps as intimations of eternity is still to be discovered."

The writers studied here are holistic thinkers whose minds rove far and wide over the intellectual products of our civilization to find evidences of the subterranean miner at work and to bring these insights home as "partners" to their own sometimes metaphorical, sometimes metaphysical visions of the primitive source of truth deep within man's mind. No literary critic has ever expressed it better than F. O. Matthiessen in *American Renaissance:*

Ahab's savagery, not unlike that of a Hebrew prophet, has rejected the warmly material pantheism of the Greeks; but Melville's breadth has effected, not a fusion, but a unique counterpoint of both. The reason why the values of both Pan and Jehovah were not merely words to him, as they are to most men, is that he had relived them for himself in his own body and mind, and especially in his imagination. This means that he had cut through the dead tissues of the culture of his day, and had rediscovered the primitive and enduring nature of man. By virtue of the range of his own experience, he was able to recognize instinctively what remained for the poet of our still more conscious age to reduce to the theory that the artist "is more *primitive*, as well as more civilized, than his contemporaries, his experience is deeper than civilization, and he only uses the phenomena of civilization in expressing it." When Eliot wrote that about Wyndham Lewis in 1918, he had just begun to tap the vital springs of anthropology in Frazer's *Golden Bough,* where he was to find the myth around which to compose *The Waste Land.* . . . In his own day Melville had enacted the same fundamental pattern by "sinking to the most primitive and forgotten, returning to the origin and bringing something back, seeking the beginning and the end." Those words of Eliot's can serve to describe the most profound level of *Moby-Dick;* and it is significant of Melville's difference from Emerson that he did not conceive of art as an ever higher and more refined ascent of the mind. He wanted nothing less than the whole of life. He symbolized its vast and terrifying forces when he likened Ahab's "darker, deeper" part to those hidden antiquities beneath the Hotel de Cluny, where man's "root of grandeur, his whole awful essence sits in bearded state." The flavor of that image is even more Biblical than Greek. It takes man beyond history to the source of his elemental energies.

A trip back to the primitive is a trip back behind civilization itself, and for this reason Melville's metaphysics is open and independent enough to encompass not just Hebrew and Christian doctrines but also such pagan oddities as cannibalism, Zoroastrianism, and Emersonian transcendentalism. Ira Progoff, in *Jung, Synchronicity, and Human Destiny,* has explained that Carl Jung's fascination with such esoteric teachings as alchemy, Zen, astrology, the *Book of the Dead,* the Tarot, and the *I Ching* arose from

his insight that, in some obscure way, they express the "underside" of human experiences. . . . All these teachings and methods were "true" in Jung's eyes in the sense that they carried a perception of reality drawn from the nonconscious and intuitive levels of the psyche. They were not "true in themselves" in the sense of being descriptions of external reality to be taken literally. But they were descriptions of the interior landscape, and to that degree were true as symbolic perceptions of a dimension of reality that can be reached only indirectly.

And so also Melville's fascination with the metaphysics preached by Ahab, that "grand, ungodly, god-like man." For Ahab speaks, because his mind has explored, the most profound language of the unconscious with all its "intimations of eternity." Melville allows him to assume "the center of the stage" over Bulkington and Starbuck not just because "he is an embodiment of his author's most profound response to the problem of the free individual will *in extremis*," as Matthiessen suggests; but because truth is as elusive as "a scared white doe in the woodlands," because fiction for Melville was "the great Art of Telling the Truth," and because the truth, therefore, needs a messenger who has freed his unconscious from civilization's notions of what is improper or heretical, who is willing to be branded "mad" as the fair exchange for earning the "manhood" that Mailer suggests eternity has to offer. Some critics, like Charles Olson, would like to redeem Melville from the taint of Ahab's "privative" vision, from his "blasphemies," all of which Melville seemed ready to accept when he wrote to Hawthorne, "I have written a wicked book, and feel as spotless as a lamb." He meant, according to Olson's *Call Me Ishmael,* that the book Ahab was writing was wicked, while he, Melville, envisions a larger "universe" and so cannot be blamed for Ahab's vision of evil. No such meaning is implicit in the statement; Melville is absolving himself for letting Ahab's demonism have the center stage for so long to the exclusion of Starbuck's orthodox Christianity and Bulkington's more serene romanticism.

Civilization, in Freud's thinking, is the systematic antagonist of the unconscious, and so a critic like Olson, whose vision of truth is born of civilization, can be expected to double-think his way around even Melville's most simply stated claims for the truth of the unconscious.

In *Life against Death* Norman O. Brown has suggested a theory of art based on Freud's *Wit and the Unconscious,* which is particularly helpful for analyzing the fiction of the writers in Mailer's second category because it emphasizes this "dialectic between art and society." The dialectic arises because the artist, like the neurotic or the dreamer, is seeking to recapture the pleasure associated with early childhood but which society, as the collective embodiment of the "reality principle" (in Freud's early formulations especially) and the "parental principle," seeks to repress: "Art, if its object is to undo repressions, and if civilization is essentially repressive, is in this sense subversive of civilization."

Brown seems to believe that literature fits very neatly into Freud's theory that wit is the socially acceptable means of making "the unconscious conscious":

Play on words—the technique of wit—is recovered when thought is allowed to sink into the unconscious. In returning to the unconscious in the quest for the materials of wit, our thoughts are only revisiting the old home where in infancy word play reigned. It takes only the reflection that metaphor, which is the building block of all poetry, is nothing but a playing with words, to see how readily Freud's analysis of wit invites extension to the whole domain of art.

But there is a further implication in this formulation. As the author repeats the forms of childish pleasure, he also repeats the primitive origins of that pleasure, because in Freud's system, according to Brown, "ontogeny recapitulates phylogeny." Freud thus came to realize, Brown says,

that the core of the neuroses of individuals [and the visions of artists] lay in the same "archaic heritage," "memory-traces of the experiences of former generations," which "can only be understood phylogenetically." The repressed unconscious which produces neurosis [and that "fine madness" literature] is not an individual unconscious but a collective one. Freud abstains from adopting Jung's term but says [in *Moses and Monotheism*], "The content of the unconscious is collective anyhow."

Freud's disciple Wilhelm Reich saw more clearly than Freud the "secret relations" between the neurotic and the artist when both become obsessed with probing the levels of the unconscious that have the most primitive and, therefore, most compelling origin. And he suggested in *Character Analysis* that the "bizarre ideas" and "mystical experiences" of paranoid schizophrenics may not always be distinguishable from the visions of "great artists"; what Mailer would later call "creative paranoia" Reich called *"the courage to approach what is commonly evaded"*:

I venture the statement that in our mental institutions many potentially great artists, musicians, scientists and philosophers are rotting away their lives because homo normalis refuses to look beyond the iron curtain which he drew in front of his real life, because he dare not look at living realities. These great souls, broken down and wrecked as "schizophrenics," KNOW and PERCEIVE what no homo normalis dares to touch. Let us not be led astray by the distortions in this knowledge. Let us listen to what these gifted and clear-visioned human beings have to say.

Roger Ramsey, in his article "Current and Recurrent: The Vietnam Novel," traces Mailer's use of Reich's case studies in evolving his own system of symbols. Mailer's use of the aurora borealis as a symbol for "God" (or at least heavenly powers) during the climactic scene of *Why Are We in Vietnam?* Ramsey believes stems from Reich's account in *Character Analysis* of the nineteenth session with a young female patient, which follows:

She searched with her eyes anxiously along the walls. Then, suddenly, she asked: "*What is the aurora borealis?* (very slowly as if with great effort) I heard about it once; there are patterns and wavy pathways in the sky . . . (she looked again searchingly along the walls of the room, as if strongly absent) . . . I hear you, I see you, but somehow far away . . . at a very great distance . . . I know very well that I am trembling now, I feel it . . . but it is not me, it is something else . . . (after a long pause). . . . I would like to get rid of this body; it is not me; *I want to be there where the 'forces' are.* . . ." [ellipses in original]

The writers studied here tell the story of characters who are either mad or clairvoyant or perhaps both, but who all share the obsessive desire to be where the forces are. It may be that in order for modern critics to understand what these writers are trying to tell us by creating these characters they will have to develop holistic habits of thought equal to those of the writers they are studying. I begin with Melville's assumption that the subterranean miner works in us all and end with Jung's assumption, as expressed by Progoff, that "for anyone who is living in close connection with his unconscious" truth of a "parapsychic type" will make itself known, whether that anyone be author, character, reader, or even critic.

But the special responsibility of the critic in analyzing fictional themes, which parallels that of the psychoanalyst when determining the implications of behavior patterns in his patient, arises from Jung's observation, as reported by Progoff, that the connection with the unconscious can be "expressed through either of its opposite forms, through the conscious development of larger cognitive capacities in a sensitive personality, or through an uncontrolled predominance of the unconscious, as in psychosis." The themes of these five writers are "descriptions of the interior landscape" and, as such, can be reached only "intuitively" and "indirectly"; thus, the critic can expect "distortions in this knowledge," but we can expect the critic to approach such fictional themes with a world view large enough and forgiving enough to know when "psychosis" is being presented as a side-effect of "larger cognitive capacities" and when it is just psychosis. Does Melville, for example, present Ahab's vision of "defiance" as "right worship" sympathetically or does he mean for the reader to pity or despise Ahab for having so distorted the nature of reality?

Such a question can have only one answer for a critic like Frederic Jameson because his world view equates individualistic "fantasies" with a kind of antisocial neurosis for which literature ought to serve "as a 'talking cure,' as a way of bringing such buried fantasies to expression in the broad daylight of social consciousness." James Dickey does not put enough "distance" (to use the terminology of Wayne C. Booth) between himself as "implied author" and the "cult of *machismo,* of maleness and courage" seemingly acceptable to the hero-narrator of *Deliverance,* which must mean, concludes Jameson, that "what is the matter with Dickey's treatment of these social terrors is that he is himself possessed by them." There is nothing wrong with Jameson's critical method here. The fact that Dickey allows Ed Gentry at the conclusion of the novel "to think of himself as bathing in the legendary glow of moderate heroism," as Jameson puts it, is clear evidence that Dickey intends for us to feel no ironic distance between Ed's perceptions of why he has triumphed and the author's convictions about why he has, in fact, triumphed. It is the second part of Jameson's conclusion about Dickey that I dispute; it seems that Dickey is not just "possessed" of a vision stridently preaching maleness and courage but is also "profoundly unconscious" of its "shaping presence" in his novel.

To say this, if we accept Jung's dialectic ("larger cognitive capacities" versus "an uncontrolled predominance of the unconscious"), is to say that Dickey is neurotic or psychotic, and, in fact, Jameson is ready to go so far as to say that the theme of *Deliverance* is "an outright political and social wish-fulfilment" which "reinforces" the most subversive of anti-social instincts in that group of subhumans Jameson pictures, one assumes, as Dickey's readers.

The clear problem is that Jameson's world view does not acknowledge that any human needs or drives or passions can be *a*political, that one can shore fragments of "maleness and courage" against the ruins of his primitive self while giving little thought to how society is going to effect its own salvation. "Surely," Jameson tells us, "such ossified inner structures" should not be revived, and he cannot see how "any good man, in his own proper character" could disagree.

2

A CARPET-BAG
FOR ETERNITY

Mining is the best metaphor for the metaphorical process itself, a powerful intellect sinking to the deepest levels of the unconscious and bringing the unrefined ore of truth to the surface of consciousness. One discovers good metaphors; one invents bad ones. The process of analogy has become increasingly important to modern physics as scientific inquiry has shifted from an observation of "concrete" mechanical laws of motion and thermodynamics and such to the nonobservable emptiness of subatomic and macrocosmic reality. In *The Universe and Dr. Einstein,* Lincoln Barnett states that metaphor was Einstein's "usual mode of creative thought" and offers as illustration the famous "elevator" analogy by which Einstein demonstrated that the traditional conception of gravity as one phenomenon and inertia as another was a matter of the relativity inherent in the human point of view. (Einstein observed that a dropping elevator on earth would duplicate for its occupants the weightlessness of outer space. Conversely, the motion of a room through outer space could duplicate for its occupants the effects of gravity.) But nobody seems to look for scientifically valid "truth" in literary metaphors. Even Arthur Koestler, himself a novelist, writing in his book on physics and parapsychology, *The Roots of Coincidence,* warns his readers not to disparage the analogy of a famous physicist as "just a poetic metaphor." The idea, he says, "goes deeper." For shame, Arthur Koestler.

In this chapter I will suggest a rationale for the clairvoyant power of the Mailer brand of visionary literature, a literature which takes the nonobservable unconcious for subject, just as there is a branch of physics which eschews the study of the concrete for the study of the nonobservable subatomic universe.

The doctrine of the "implicit analogue," which emphasizes the interdependence of analogy and scientific method and of "intuition" and empiricism, is at the center of M. H. Abrams's *The Mirror and the Lamp,* an analysis of Western literary history:

Any area for investigation, so long as it lacks prior concepts to give it structure and an express terminology with which it can be managed, appears to the inquiring mind inchoate—either a blank, or an elusive and tantalizing confusion. Our usual recourse is, more or less deliberately, to cast about for objects which offer parallels to dimly sensed aspects of the new situation, to use the better known to elucidate the less known, to discuss the intangible in terms of the tangible. This analogical procedure seems characteristic of much intellectual enterprise. There is a deal of wisdom in the popular locution for "What is its nature?" namely: "What's it *like?"* We tend to describe the nature of something in similes and metaphors, and the vehicles of these recurrent figures, when analyzed, often turn out to be the attributes of an implicit analogue through which we are viewing the object we describe. And if I am right, Plato's deliberate use of analogue and parable differs from that of many other inquirers less in tactics than in candor.

It was "changing metaphors of mind," according to Abrams, that facilitated the romantic revolution, allowing man once more to conceive of his mind as an active agent of a universe that the rationalists had tried to separate into object and subject, matter and mind, organic and mechanistic but that was once again whole:

It was . . . an attempt to overcome the sense of man's alienation from the world by healing the cleavage between subject and object, between the vital, purposeful, value-full world of private experience and the dead postulated world of extension, quantity, and motion. To establish that man shares his own life with nature was to reanimate the dead universe of the materialists, and at the same time most effectively to tie man back into his milieu.

If anything unites the writers in this study, it is their common attempt to "reanimate the dead universe" by envisioning the inner connections of man's mind with his "milieu," but they go beyond the European romantics by wanting to identify and classify these connections systematically and even scientifically. Indeed, Norman O. Brown has suggested that much of what modern man tends to interpret as sheer mysticism in an ancient writer like Plato may simply be an analogical expression of a now scientifically verified theory of the unconscious: "The Freudian doctrine of the archetypal status of childhood [in the unconscious] can put the Platonic doctrine of anamnesis on a naturalistic basis." The logic of Poe's metaphysics, for example, rests on assumptions completely opposite from those of more traditional romantics like Emerson and Whitman. In *Symbolism and American Literature* Charles Feidelson explains the difference:

The ambiguity of Poe's metaphysics, which constitutes a kind of materialistic idealism, exactly corresponds to the paradox of "process." The psychophysical world projected by the transcendentalists might be called an idealistic materialism. But, instead of attempting to describe the unity of thought and things from the side of "spirit," Poe carries out the same unification in terms of matter, infinitely rarefied "until we arrive at a matter *unparticled*–without particles–indivisible–one." His purpose is not reduction of one term to the other but reconciliation: "The matter of which I speak is, in all respects, the very 'mind' or 'spirit' of the schools . . . and is, moreover, the 'matter' of these schools at the same time."

In an article in *Poe Studies* Harriet R. Holman claims that Poe's *Eureka* (1848), from which Feidelson takes the quotations above, is not a reliable guide to Poe's metaphysics since, she says, it was obviously written as a satire on "arm-chair science." Secure in her commission of the intentional fallacy, she is less impressed by what Poe "foresaw" of twentieth-century physics than by the internal evidence she finds of factual errors so glaring that Poe must have been joking. However, secure in my emotional commitment to Brown's theory that Freud's analysis of jokes can be made into a theory of art, I am more impressed by what Poe's probing of his unconscious taught him about twentieth-century physics than I am disturbed by his errors. The analogy that Koestler urges his readers not to dismiss as a *mere* "poetic metaphor" is contained in the physicist Sir James Jeans's famous statement, "The stream of knowledge is heading towards a non-mechanical reality; the universe begins to look more like a great thought than like a great machine." This is exactly what Poe proposed, and Poe's concept of "imparticularity" seems the parallel of what Koestler calls the "post-materialistic trend in modern physics." Koestler reports that, as the physicists of this century were forced to abandon one theory of the basic constituents of matter after another, they were finally forced to conclude that "its ultimate constituents" are not "'things' but processes." Poe, whose metaphysics "exactly corresponds to the paradox of 'process'" and who uses his own terms for the fields of force which Einstein would later postulate as underlying all material reality (Poe's "system of *cycles*" and "Universal irradiation" seem to anticipate Einstein's Unified Field Theory), makes a formulation in *Eureka* exactly parallel to Koestler's: "Matter *exists* only as attraction and repulsion . . . attraction and repulsion *are* matter."

Poet as scientist, scientist as poet; both perhaps are mining their insights from the same mother lode, some universal system of implicit analogues into which the individual unconscious is keyed and by which the individual conscious mind, through contemplation of the unconscious, can transcend its limitations to receive a vision of the whole. Koestler uses imagery similar to Melville's, which should no longer be surprising, to postulate "a subterranean pool" at the core of all thought, which draws its power from "the fundamental unity of all things, transcending mechanical causality," and which, therefore, can be used as a working hypothesis for an ultimate scientific explanation of ESP, ancient systems of divination (e.g., the *I Ching*), and the roots of coincidence:

The classical theories of ESP proposed by Carington, Tyrell, Hardy and others were variations on the same theme—a "psychic ether" [now called "psi" after the equally nonmaterial "psi fields" of modern quantum mechanics] or group-mind or collective unconscious, serving as a subterranean pool which individual minds can tap, and through which they can communicate. The dominant concept is Unity in Diversity—all is One and One is all. It echoes through the writings of Christian mystics, and is the keynote in Buddhism and Taoism. It provides the parallels of latitude on Schopenhauer's globe, and ties coincidence into the universal scheme of things. According to Jung, all divinatory practices, from looking at tea-leaves to the complicated oracular methods of the *I Ching,* are based on the idea that random events are minor mysteries which can be used as pointers towards the one central mystery.

And Melville understood that it is precisely this "central mystery" that the sensitive reader looks for in a work of art; it and not the niceties of structure and style is the force that makes a work resonate at the deepest levels of the reader's mind, that gives form to the whole:

Whence come you, Hawthorne? By what right do you drink from my flagon of life? and when I put it to my lips—lo, they are yours and not mine. I feel that the Godhead is broken up like the bread at the Supper, and that we are the pieces. Hence this infinite fraternity of feeling. Now, sympathizing with the paper, my angel turns over another page. You did not care a penny for the book. But, now and then as you read, you understood the pervading *thought* that impelled the book—and that you praised. Was it not so? You were archangel enough to despise the imperfect body, and embrace the soul. Once you hugged the ugly Socrates because you saw the flame in the mouth, and heard the rushing of the *demon,*—the familiar,—and recognized the sound; for you have heard it in your own solitudes. [my italics]

The reunification of thought and matter "in terms of matter" (Feidelson's phrase) is one of the projects of contemporary physics, according to Koestler. A "mad" project, Koestler concedes, but only because modern physicists have had to learn to live with mad, contradictory principles that madden mostly because they work. Physicists have seen their beloved "cause and effect" succumb to "acausal" principles like the statistical "law of large numbers" and Werner Heisenberg's "uncertainty principle." So physicists are more ready than the layman to accept the reality of extrasensory mental powers (telepathy, precognition, clairvoyance, retrocognition, and psychokinesis) because they know that the senses lie. Our senses tell us that we live in a stable, solid, deterministic universe in which matter is more real than what cannot be seen or felt, but mathematical formulas tell us that we live in a "shadow" universe in which mass is energy and energy, mass. And that either can sometimes act as matter and at other times as energy wave, that not only is matter mostly empty but that the unbounded emptiness may in fact be a totally inconceivable "bottomless sea of electrons with *negative mass*" (Paul Dirac's theory as described by Koestler).

The reunification of thought and matter, as Poe predicted, is accomplished because matter as we know it through the senses is an extension of some unsubstantial subatomic process which forms an analogue to mental process too implicit to be mere coincidence (mere coincidence to the layman, "meaningful" coincidence to Jung and Koestler). As Koestler explains:

The contents of conscious experience have no spatio-temporal dimensions; in this respect they resemble the non-things of quantum physics which also defy definition in terms of space, time and substance—or, to quote Jeans again, can only be described "by going outside space and time." But the unsubstantial contents of consciousness are somehow linked with the substantial brain; and the physicist's unsubstantial psi fields are somehow linked with the substantial aspects of material particles. This is the parallel implied in Heisenberg's remark that the Copenhagen complementarity of corpuscle and wave [that is, Niels Bohr's "principle of complementarity"] and the Cartesian dualism of matter and mind, agree with each other "very neatly"; and in Jeans's remark that the universe looks more like a thought than a machine. "More" and not "equally" —because both in Einstein's cosmos and the sub-atomic micro-cosmos, the non-substantial aspects dominate; in both, matter dissolves into energy, energy into shifting configurations of something unknown. Eddington summed it up in his epigram: "The stuff of the world is mind-stuff." The hard, tangible appearance of things exists only in our medium-sized world measured in pounds and yards, to which our senses are attuned. On both the cosmic and the sub-atomic scale this intimate, tangible relationship turns out to be an illusion.

With the writings of Jung and Reich emerges a new notion of the unconscious as the respository of powers that Freud merely hinted at, and, if we can believe them, a deeper understanding of why the inward-looking American novel tends to be more "profound" and "clairvoyant" than the outer-directed, sense-experience English novel. Jung postulated that the archetypes (principally, the shadow, the anima, and the animus) to be found at the depths of the "collective unconscious" are linked in some acausal way to the pattern of the unseen universe, and, therefore, archetypal experiences or the experience of archetypes in some personal way facilitate, or interact with, the parapsychological phenomena that history shows as often accompanying intense emotions. Ira Progoff explains it this way:

The effective point of linkage is at the archetypal level. The specific archetypes that are active at the depth of the individual's existence are the means by which the general orderedness of the larger patterns of the macrocosm can come to specific expression at any moment of time. The archetypes are the vehicles by which the encompassing patterns of life are individualized in experience, and Synchronicity is the explanatory principle by which the chance and meaning of the intersection of these experiences in time may be recognized and comprehended. . . . The archetypes alone hold the possibility of bringing about a connection via psychic experience between the individual human being and the non-causal ordering principle. On the other hand, since the archetype is itself an expression of the pattern, its "effect" on surrounding events is to draw them into conformity with the pervading principle.

Koestler does not accept all of Jung's theory, because of its vestiges of causality in the relationship drawn between archetypes and parapsychological phenomena. But he is ready to accept, because recent research in physics and parapsychology has demonstrated, one, that parapsychological experiences have their roots in the unconscious (Sir Cyril Burt and Professor H. H. Price of Oxford theorize, for example, that ESP mechanisms are screened by the musculature and conscious mind to such an extent that they must make themselves conscious by means of the very same devices as other archetypal unconscious impulses: "symbolic form," "hallucinations," "dreams," and "automatic writing"); and, two, that there is indeed a noncausal ordering principle in the universe something like Jung's synchronicity or Kammerer's "seriality" with which the unconscious is attuned (he calls it "confluence" because of the unfortunate tendency of the other two terms to emphasize the confluence of events in time to the exclusion of correspondence in space). And he is prepared to link the unconscious to various Western "cosmologies" through the "a-causal" principle; the cosmologies becoming in this view symbolic pictures drawn by the unconscious, "descriptions of the interior landscape" in the form of pictures of the external landscape, imaging finally the ineffable connections of macrocosmos and microcosmos, of universal mind and individual mind, of body and mind, of matter and process:

Both Kammerer and Jung postulate an a-causal principle which they consider of equal importance with causality in the destiny of man and of the world at large. The paradoxes of quantum physics may suggest that this postulate is no more preposterous than the theorems of modern science; but even if we were prepared to accept it, we would at once be compelled to ask: what is that a-causal agency up to? . . .

From antiquity until about the eighteenth century, men had a ready answer to that question in terms of "influences," "sympathies" and "correspondences." The constellations of the planets governed man's character and destiny; macro-cosmos was reflected in micro-cosmos; everything was hanging together, not by mechanical causes but by hidden affinities; there was no room for coincidences in that invisible order. . . . It runs like a *leitmotif* through the teaching of the Pythagoreans, the Neo-Platonists and the philosophers of the Renaissance. The dualism of causality and a-causal "sympathy." . . .

The Pythagorean concept of the Harmony of the Spheres, revived by the Elizabethans, and the philosophy underlying the pursuits of astrology and alchemy, can all be regarded as variations on the same theme: meaningful coincidences are manifestations of an all-embracing universal order. . . .

Koestler is prepared, moreover, to put this whole thing "on a naturalistic basis." With the discovery of the "neutrino" in 1956, predicted by Wolfgang Pauli in the early thirties, an elementary particle having none of the properties of matter ("no mass, no electric charge, no magnetic field" in Koestler's description), physicists began to consider seriously, according to Koestler, that the division between mind and body might prove to be just as illusory as the division between energy and mass:

The absence of "gross" physical properties in the neutrino, and its quasi-ethereal character, encouraged speculations about the possible existence of other particles which would provide the missing link between matter and mind. Thus the eminent astronomer V. A. Firsoff suggested that "mind was a universal entity or interaction of the same order as electricity or gravitation, and that there must exist a *modulus of transformation,* analogous to Einstein's famous equality $E=mc^2$ [the principle of atomic bombs and reactors, by which matter is transmuted into inconceivable amounts of energy], whereby 'mind stuff' could be equated with other entities of the physical world." He further suggested that there may exist elementary particles of the mind-stuff, which he proposed to call "mindons," with properties somewhat similar to the neutrino's.

And Adrian Dobbs, according to Koestler, postulated similar particles, based on his theory of a second time dimension (hence, a five-dimensional universe) operating by "probabilistic" rather than causal principles, in an effort to find a scientific basis for precognition:

Dobbs uses the term "pre-cast" instead of "precognition," to indicate that it refers not to prophecy, but to the perception of probabilistic factors in a system which predispose it toward a given future state. . . . Information about ["dispositional factors"] is conveyed to the subject by hypothetical messengers which Dobbs calls "psitrons" and which operate in his second time dimension. They are particles with rather startling attributes, but not much more startling than Pauli's neutrino, Dirac's minus-mass electrons, or Feynman's electrons traveling back in time—each of which brought a Nobel Prize. Dobbs's concept of the psitron is, in fact, the joint product of current trends in quantum theory and brain research. It has *imaginary* mass (in the mathematical sense) and thus, according to Relativity Theory, can travel faster than light indefinitely, without loss of (imaginary) momentum.

All of this goes much farther than Freud in putting Plato's anamnesis or Coleridge's "understanding" on a naturalistic basis. William York Tindall has written in *The Literary Symbol* that the ancient Hermetic formula "as above, so below" has been replaced for twentieth-century romantics by the Freudian notion "as in, so out" (Freud's doctrine of projection); but we have to go beyond Freud to sense, as the mystics always have, the limitlessness of the unconscious. For, as modern physicists rely more and more on abstract metaphoric systems in order to conceptualize the inconceivable, the barrier between metaphysics and physics, says Koestler, breaks down:

...we know less and less about more and more. That applies to the complementary process of the unification of matter and energy, particle and waves into one conceptual river delta, majestically moving into an ocean of abstractions—for the more precise knowledge science acquired, the more elusive became the symbols it had to use. The hunting of the quark [the entity which M. Gell-Mann postulates as underlying all the "elementary" particles] begins to resemble the mystic's quest for the cloud of unknowing.

Koestler savors the irony in the fact that parapsychology has become "acceptable" to the scientific community only as physics has become more "occult." And he affirms that this merging of the laws underlying the mind with those underlying the "material" universe

is an important step towards the demolition of the greatest superstition of our age—the materialistic clockwork universe of early-nineteenth-century physics. "To assert that there is *only matter* and no mind," Firsoff wrote, "is the most illogical of propositions, quite apart from the findings of modern physics, which show that there is no matter in the traditional meaning of the term."

Literary critics beware! A rationalistic, clockwork system of evaluation may not always be adequate to an appreciation of visionary fiction. In his review for the *New Republic* (10 April 1970), Charles Thomas Samuels applies cause-and-effect principles to *Deliverance* with an insight equal to that of Frederic Jameson. Like Jameson, Samuels sees Dickey postulating Ed Gentry's reversion to "animalism" as the cause of his "deliverance." But this confuses Samuels since the only time Ed actually uses the word "deliverance" is after intercourse with his wife, and in reference to an encounter with an attractive model who has a gold spot in her eye. But if sex causes deliverance, asks Samuels, why does the narrator go off to the woods with the boys, instead of off to have an affair with the model? Projecting his own confusions onto Dickey, he declares that it is because Dickey himself has an "ambivalence" toward both animalism and sex (which Samuels infers from Ed's appreciation for Lewis's muscular body, or something). But Samuels has an unconscious just like the rest of us which keeps breaking into his review to ask questions like "Is this reading correct?" and to tell him that of course it cannot be correct; nothing involving unconscious motivations is ever that simple. Complexity, not ambivalence, is the nature of the vision. Dickey knows that a simple return to nature cannot cause the return to wholeness that Ed experiences, as the unregenerate presence of the two demented mountain men makes clear; it is a return to wholeness, body to mind and mind to universe, which cannot be willed into being, and if animalism finds its implicit analogue in the sex act, it is so because in neither case can the unconscious instincts, either atavistic or sexual, be willed into arousal.

Dickey would appreciate Koestler's observation that E SP like sex always involves "some self-transcending type of emotion," in Grey Walter's words "a paradoxical compound of detachment and excitement," which cannot be turned on and off like a tap. "Our inability to control the unconscious processes underlying" E SP, Koestler suggests, accounts for its "erratic nature." But E SP occurrences can be facilitated by the ambience in which they occur. Koestler, commenting on Jung's theory of how archetypes interact with paranormal experience, says:

The "decisive factors" in the collective unconscious are the archetypes which "constitute its structure." They are, as it were, the distilled memories of the human species, but cannot be represented in verbal terms, only in elusive symbols, shared by all mythologies. They also provide "patterns of behavior" for all human beings in archetypal situations—confrontations with death, danger, love, conflict, etc. In such situations the unconscious archetypes invade consciousness, carrying strong emotions and—owing perhaps to the archetype's indifference to physical space and time—facilitate the occurrence of "synchronistic" events.

Ed does appear to experience both telepathy (when he feels his mind "merge" with that of the evil mountain man) and psychokinesis (when his hand seems to "split" a crevice in the face of the cliff) during his "confrontation" with danger and death, but the narrator does not celebrate, or even mention again, these new-found powers as though they bore with them any saving grace. What he does emphasize over and over again is that the archetypal situation brings with it its own "patterns of behavior." There are no moral choices to make; one just goes with the flow. "We were all acting it out," he says during his climb up the cliff. This theme appears also in the work of Norman Mailer, especially in *Why Are We in Vietnam?* One either finds himself tuned-in to nature's circuits or one does not. One can will to live in the wilderness, but one cannot will the deliverance that may be nurtured by it. We may not like the dialectic underlying natural process any more than the dialectic underlying society (both of which may, of course, participate in the same all-pervading principles), but the tentative conclusion of Mailer's narrator, D. J., is that it is better to live by the dictates of one's innate defecation impulses than by the "plastic asshole" issued by society, which is a metaphoric way of expressing Norman O. Brown's scatological interpretation of civilized history, which is in turn a way of saying that society, as a rigid system of repressions and sublimations of primal instinctual processes, is "designed precisely to drive men deep into onanism and homosexuality."

Koestler postulates a "psycho-magnetic field" as the principle underlying "confluent events," a principle which bears a startling resemblance to a key "metaphor" in Mailer's novel: "the undiscovered magnetic-electro fief of the dream, which is opposed to the electromagnetic field of the earth just as properly as the square root of minus one is opposed to one." But more significant than the prophetic power of Mailer's imagination or the naturalistic, scientific foundations of his metaphysics is the vision brought back from the upper reaches of the inner Amazon that "it all flows, mind and asshole, anode and cathode, you sending messages and receiving all through the night." Sex does not cause deliverance and neither does atavism, but both Dickey and Mailer share the insight, made obvious by the compulsions of their heroes, that murder, as Mailer has said on television to Gore Vidal's distaste, is a sexual act and that murder, therefore, must be recognized by Paul Goodman's generation as being at least as legitimate a path to self-transcendence as guilt-free sex.

Letting the conscious mind flow into the unconscious, what D. J. calls "the spook flux of the night," and learning to bring something articulate back, is how the visionary writer values his work, because, just as "mining" is the best metaphor for how they work, how they work gives them the sense that they are involved in purposes not strictly their own, as the comment by Melville above (p. 25) or the following comment from Dickey's *Playboy* interview (November 1973) makes clear:

Alcohol or heroin or whatever is nothing compared with the burst of glory that descends from the clouds when you say something that you didn't know you could say and it's just damn good. That's the only rule of thumb I have for judging anything I write: It's good when I say something I hadn't any idea my mind was capable of producing.

But Mailer, more sentimental than Dickey or maybe just tired of being the messenger murdered for his bad news, would like to bring the critics into the flow, relieve them of the burden of their clockwork superstitions, and introduce them to the new science. I like to think that he has critics like Jameson, Yurick, and Samuels in mind when he has D. J. give this advice:

D. J., Grand Synthesizer of the Modern Void, suggests that the intellectual equipment to comprehend why frustration makes crystals of impulse when they are in the mode of liquid chemical matter is not yet yours. Study basic electricity, basic electronics. Come back. D. J. will stick an electrode up your ass.

3

DUMB BRUTES AS
PASTEBOARD MASKS

Our literature reflects the tone of our ironic age, the age of pessimistic determinism, existential despair, black humor, the novel of the absurd; no longer are human aspirations to be taken quite seriously, no longer can the human will be granted power commensurate with its desires. The naturalistic movement in modern literature would seem to have killed forever the romantic dream, would seem to have paved the way for the existentialists' last stand, replacing the romantic image of a man with his fingertips on the harp strings of heaven with the image of a man digging with swine fingers for the pearls that may or may not have been cast before him. Norman Mailer in *The Naked and the Dead* has captured in miniature the essence of the naturalistic plot in his description of Pvt. Roth's fatal fall from a mountain ledge:

In his fall Roth heard himself bellow with anger, and was amazed that he could make so great a noise. Through his numbness, through his disbelief, he had a thought before he crashed into the rocks below. He wanted to live. A little man, tumbling through space.

The tragedy of the little man, victim of an ironically small misstep, hurling an inarticulate protest at a void badly in need of a synthesizer; we know the "dumb brute" story well.

Einstein's physics teaches that space is not empty but, as

Koestler puts it, teeming with "stresses, warps, or kinks," that space is not formless, therefore, but curved, that if one could travel through space, as James A. Coleman explains it in *Relativity for the Layman,* in a "straight line" long enough, one would eventually find himself back at the point where he started. Similarly, Northrop Frye's *Anatomy of Criticism* teaches that the straight line that Western fiction has followed, from ancient heroic myth to contemporary pathetic irony, as Western man has come to think less and less of himself, is endless only in the sense that the line curves back upon its beginning. Why? That is the nature of things.

Some critics such as Robert Scholes in *Structuralism in Literature* would like to liberate Frye's "fictional chronology" from its "myth of eternal return," without realizing that it is Frye's vision of the "circle" that animates what Scholes calls "the diachronic thrust of his presentation." Frye has presented the hypothesis, and it is time to stop defying its conclusions and start testing it against the patterns to be found in our fiction. We began with a heavily metaphorical story, the myth, a story involving characters serving as "pasteboard masks," as Melville put it, or as "projections" of archetypal relationships, as Frye puts it in *Fables of Identity.* We have been passing through a period in which "the need to tell a credible or plausible story" has inhibited the storyteller from presenting his characters as anything but "dumb brutes," minus the suggestions of a mysterious subterranean level of multiplying significances. And we appear now to have passed the nadir of the circle; out of the ashes of a total renunciation of human worth has arisen phoenix-like a new vision of godlike, mythic man. And so we arrive back at a heavily metaphorical fiction in which the actions of any character spread outward and inward into eternal significances. The trouble is, as Laura Adams points out in *Will the Real Norman Mailer Please Stand Up,* that the critics are still fixated on "dumb brute" realism:

To seek victory over what one considers evil and productive of death is to strive toward the heroic condition. Convinced of the need for a heroic leader, a man capable of embodying the ambiguities and contradictions of this discordant age, Mailer began to develop him through the contours of style. That style has always been heavily metaphorical, and attempts to take him literally have often obscured his meaning. The initial reception of *An American Dream* is a case in point. Read as realism, the book seems to justify murder and sexual perversion [in a note Professor Adams cites the negative responses of literary critics Elizabeth Hardwick and Philip Rahv] . However, as a metaphor for America's need to rid itself of its corruption and to seek a new and better self truer to the old American Dream, the novel is one of the finest contemporary visions of America's possibility through a courageous and radical heroism.

Ralph Ellison has a mysterious black veteran, who happens to be both a brain surgeon and "an inmate of a semi-madhouse," tell the invisible man what might be a good principle for critics to learn:

". . . for God's sake, learn to look beneath the surface. . . . Come out of the fog, young man. . . . Play the game, but play it your own way—part of the time at least. Play the game, but raise the ante, my boy. Learn how it operates, learn how *you* operate. . . . You might even beat the game. It's really a very crude affair. Really Pre-Renaissance—and that game has been analyzed, put down in books."

He is saying that society has a structure, rules, and that our social fates are determined by how well we have analyzed the rules. Keep a person ignorant of the laws of probability and you have created the perfect poker partner, which is something like what white society has done to blacks, Ellison suggests.

Literature also has an underlying structure, "an order of words," Northrop Frye says in *Fables of Identity,* "corresponding to the order of nature." All narratives within sophisticated literature are "displacements" of myth; and narrative is the literary equivalent of natural "rhythm":

Rhythm, or recurrent movement, is deeply founded on the natural cycle, and everything in nature that we think of as having some analogy with works of art, like the flower or the bird's song, grows out of a profound *synchronization* between an organism and the rhythms of its environment, especially that of the solar year. With animals some expressions of synchronization, like the mating dances of birds, could almost be called rituals. But in human life a ritual seems to be something of a voluntary effort (hence the magical element in it) to recapture a lost rapport with the natural cycle. . . . In ritual, then, we may find the origin of narrative, a ritual being a temporal sequence of acts in which the conscious meaning is latent. . . . [my italics]

Frye identifies the "single pattern of significance" in fiction as "the quest myth," and his notion of ritual as a quasi-magical effort to "recapture a lost rapport with the natural cycle" (similar to Freud's theory of the "repetition compulsion" as the grounding of all instincts) suggests something of its psychological force. But the literary critic, like Ellison's invisible man, must teach himself to "look beneath" this surface pattern to the laws governing what Frye calls "the workings of the subconscious where the epiphany originates, in other words in the dream."

I have said that I am trying to map an intellectual tradition in American fiction (p. 7), and Frye's dynamic suggests something of what I mean. The narratives studied here are all framed by a dramatized narrator (either as "protagonist-narrator" or "witness-narrator," to use Norman Friedman's terminology) in such a way as to make clear the naturally ordained dialectic between thinking and feeling, between the conscious and the unconscious. The frameworks are all extremely elaborate and formal intellectualizations on what Frye calls "the meaning or significance" (dianoia) of the pattern or "structure" (mythos) of the framed narrative. Ishmael, the sailor-hero of "A Descent into the Maelstrom," the invisible man, D.J., Stephen Rojack, and Ed Gentry each goes to extremes to tell the reader how he happened to find himself in the epic situation and what he has concluded about it. In *Fables of Identity* Frye observes that

. . . in the direct experience of fiction, continuity is the center of our attention; our later memory, or what I call the possession of it, tends to become discontinuous. Our attention shifts from the sequence of incidents to another focus; a sense of what the work of fiction was all *about*, or what criticism usually calls its theme.

These writers have to some extent taken the critical function unto themselves; they want it both ways, both to show and to tell, both to feel and to think. Perhaps at a primal level they feel that the flow of words, like Max Planck's stream of radiation, consists of both continuous wave and discontinuous quanta;

perhaps they do not trust the critics fully to appreciate the structuring power of the dream fief; or, perhaps, as Ellison's vet-surgeon-madman suggests, they are trying to "raise the ante" and even "beat" the mythos game.

That last takes some explaining. The discontinuous process that Frye describes seems the exact equivalent of the structuralist method that Claude Lévi-Strauss applies to primitive myths. Lévi-Strauss, like Frye, is concerned with isolating what Lévi-Strauss calls "the true constituent units of a myth," and he realizes with Frye that isolating the "bundles" of motifs or relationships that make up the myth's "shortest possible sentences" (by analogy with grammatical structure) can be done only by separating these motifs from the narrative rhythms in which they occur. Lévi-Strauss does this by grouping the motifs according to principles of mathematics and musical harmony, totally disregarding the sequential chain of cause-and-effect that E. M. Forster's *Aspects of the Novel* enshrined as the essence of narrative plot, and by this discontinuous systematizing Lévi-Strauss demonstrates that the unconscious obsessions structuring the narrative rhythm are often not what the cause-and-effect relations of the plot make them appear. For example, the plot of the Oedipus myth would seem to mirror mankind's obsessive fear of violating certain social taboos like patricide and incest and thus offending the gods to such an extent that the delicate harmony between heaven and society is upset, with calamitous results for society. But, in fact, if I draw correct implications from Lévi-Strauss's analysis in "The Structural Study of Myth" (1955), what structures the myth is mankind's obsessive fear that society and heaven are forever out of synchronization and what foredooms Oedipus is the vanity in attempting to build what cannot be successfully built, a lawful society.

Lévi-Strauss groups the motifs into four columns, in which one is to two as three is to four: one, "the overrating of blood relations" (Oedipus marries his mother), two, "the underrating of blood relations" (Oedipus kills his father), three, "the denial of the autochthonous origin of man" (Cadmus kills the dragon, a chthonian being, so he can build his city; Oedipus outwits the Sphinx and ascends to the throne and his mother's bed), four, "difficulties to walk and behave straight" (the name "Oedipus" means "swollen-foot"). Lévi-Strauss concludes:

> The myth has to do with the inability, for a culture which holds the belief that mankind is autochthonous . . . , to find a satisfactory transition between this theory and the knowledge that human beings are actually born from the union of man and woman . . . born from one or born from two? born from different or born from same? By a correlation of this type, the overrating of blood relations is to the underrating of blood relations as the attempt to escape autochthony is to the impossibility to succeed in it. Although experience [apparently the experiencing of sex and procreation] contradicts theory, social life verifies the cosmology by its similarity of structure. Hence cosmology is true.

The first two columns, I believe, represent the origins of civilized man, and the second two represent the cosmology that connects man's origins to the vegetation cycle; the first column represents the desire to believe that man and his society are self-perpetuating by virtue of society's fundamental link to nature, the mother; the second, the fear that the social contract cannot succeed (patricide suggests not just rebellion but a compulsive fixation on the "one" and the "same": the mother); the third, the desire of the intellect to be free to build its own world or society (i.e., the city); the fourth, the unconscious understanding that however much man's unique mind may soar, his animal body is forever "tethered with an iron ring" (as in the Prometheus myth) to the earth. But Lévi-Strauss's conclusion seems backwards; the social life does not verify the cosmology; the cosmology, when understood, verifies and articulates what the unconscious has been telling us all along about social experience: that society fails because it is built upon an illusion. Nothing articulates this better than the fact that reverence for the mother is all bound up with the motif of incest in the myth; it was Freud who first pointed out that the incest taboo, by making the family possible, is the bedrock upon which society is built; even column one denies three.

To say this is to shift the focus of Freud's "Oedipal project" from the individual psyche to the cosmology in which it is born (Lévi-Strauss himself declares that Freud's use of the myth is as "authentic" as any of the early recorded versions).

The desire we might attribute to the child to possess the mother and remove the threat of the father might better be seen as a metaphorical rendering of the unconscious desire of a human being to return to his autochthonic, natural origins (union with the mother) in spite of the threat of sanction held by society (the father). Robert Graves, whose *The White Goddess* (1947) antedates Frye's efforts to link literature to myth, and myth, in Graves's words, to "tree-lore," suggests that, sometime in the development of early civilization, the fertility goddesses of primitive religion "who presided over all acts of generation whatsoever" were deposed by the classical gods of a "new religion of logic," the death of mother worship being a necessary first-step in the building of society. The dynamic is clear: birth out of one to birth out of two, the claims of maternity to the claims of paternity, the claims of the earth to the claims of society, union to division, peace to tension, unconscious urging to conscious proposition, the natural order versus social order. And poetry, according to Graves, when it is really poetry, is the "magical language" born of the subconscious project to "invoke" the moon-goddess of the fertility cycle, to the exclusion of logic or the social good. It is not surprising to learn, as Graves has affirmed in his Oxford lectures, that *The White Goddess* was originally rejected by a legion of socially responsible publishers.

But the key to understanding mankind's inability "to find a satisfactory transition" between the cosmological and the social is that "experience" is grounded in the "senses," while cosmology is grounded in the unconscious. Koestler has demonstrated that the senses are tuned "to the hard, tangible appearance of things" which "exists only in our medium-sized world." Society exists in this world and operates by laws dictated by sense experience, and the senses tell us that, if a child is born of a woman following sexual union with a man, the man's part must be the causative factor. But the unconscious is tuned to the acausal harmony of the subatomic and macrocosmic universe, and the unconscious knows that the claims of the father are so tenuous compared to the mother's life-nurturing body that heaven could easily do without the father (as in the Christian myth of the Virgin Mother) and, by implication, the father's social logic. Society responds by creating what Norman O. Brown calls "super-organic culture," which is designed to perpetuate "the revolt against organic dependence on the mother," and which works by allowing the individual to keep his Oedipal yearnings in a desexualized, perpetually unsatisfactory, tormented form. Biological imperative is sublimated into longings for religious experience and cultural achievement, according to Brown, and what society cannot afford to accomplish in physical fact, it effects psychologically: castration.

The storyteller raises the ante when he realizes the profound antagonism between the pseudorationalism in which society is born and the seeming irrationality by which the unconscious works, and so, in a manner similar to structuralist method, he shakes his motifs free of their narrative rhythms and analyzes them before the critics can get to the work with their clockwork superstitions and the cries of "decadence" which are their chief contribution to the self-perpetuation of society. The critics come bearing talismans that protect them from seeing anything beneath the surface that might undermine their faith in civilization's ability to save man from his animal roots, when, in fact, if there is any saving to be done, it is man from his civilization.

Ralph Ellison's *Invisible Man* is a case in point. Ellison shares the distinction with Mailer of being a lapsed socialist (Sol Yurick says he is not ready to "forgive" Mailer for his betrayal of leftist causes; he probably will never forgive Ellison either. Alas, poor Yurick!), and his book has inspired hostility from the very group one would expect to be its strongest supporters: the Marxist-oriented black activist movement. This probably stems from the fact that, while the book confirms brilliantly many of their deepest convictions about the white racist power structure, it also denies the validity of social reform (or "revolution" in Marxist terms). Black activists cannot forgive the invisible man for seeking to murder their hero Ras the Destroyer, but the final vision of the invisible man is that the social good is hollow at its core, that society is merely a game to be played; rules need to be learned but not to be taken seriously. The hero's ability to win the game rests upon his readiness to remain an "isolate agonist," to murder the man, be he dumb brute or pasteboard mask, agent or principal, who would rob him of his natural identity. In this light the need to murder Moby Dick, the desire to "dismember" one's "dismemberer," the need to escape the father's punishing power, appears as an act of affirmation. As the invisible man says before hurling his spear at his personal Moby Dick, Ras,

that I, a little black man with an assumed name should die because a big black man in his hatred and confusion over the nature of a reality that seemed controlled solely by white men whom I knew to be as blind as he [*sic*], was just too much, too outrageously absurd. And I knew that it was better to live out one's own absurdity than to die for that of others. . . .

Ras's "confusion" spreads outward to the critics. Edward Margolies in *Native Sons* concludes that "no social message, no system of beliefs, no intellectual conclusions" are arrived at in the invisible man's tale. The prologue and the epilogue, certainly not standard novelistic devices these days, are such obvious reminders of the novel's intellectual framework that one cannot help but wonder about a critic's motives in denying its existence. The invisible man's "discontinuous" insights into the structure of society come to him through the interpretations of symbolic dreams, the three most important having to do with the standard Freudian themes of incest, patricide, and castration. In the final, most terrifying dream, the invisible man declares himself free of the "illusions" of society, only to be castrated by all the father figures, pasteboard masks, he has encountered on his odyssey back into his unconscious: Emerson, Bledsoe, Norton, Ras, and especially his old Marxist comrade Brother Jack. He awakes to find that, in spite of the dream, he is "whole," body and mind, and his concluding "social message" is to "never lose sight of the chaos against which" mankind conceives patterns for living. "How to be!" is the question that the invisible man seeks to answer, the same question which, according to Joseph Conrad's Stein, Lord Jim pursues. But now, perhaps, Ellison has suggested a little more of the necessary connection between Stein's two rules:

"To follow the dream, and again to follow the dream" and "In the destructive element immerse."

"Upping the ante," as Norman Mailer has said to Laura Adams in an interview conducted for *Partisan Review,* is a process of the "wicked" (as opposed to "evil" in Mailer's terminology) project of the writer to get the cosmos to yield up its secrets about the complex connection between "good and evil" in the universe. And part of the project involves learning to trust that there is a similarity between the structure of social life and the cosmology used to symbolize it, between the pasteboard mask and the "inscrutable malice sinewing it," that is too harmonious to be merely coincidental or arbitrary. The metaphorical language of myth "may be mad," as Koestler says of quantum physics, "but it has method, and it works." Some critics appear to be a step behind Adams in their interpretation of Mailer's metaphorical style, but it appears from Adams's recent exchange with Mailer that she had been a step behind Mailer. The "dumb brute" critics began with the assumptions of realism; the "pasteboard mask" critic has her own assumptions; and Mailer himself appears to have arrived back at a purely realistic aesthetic:

INT.: But it's a highly metaphorical novel. One of the mistakes many critics made in first reviewing it was to take it too literally. Isn't Cherry [in *An American Dream*] seen metaphorically as love, the reward of courage?

MAILER: Well, no. I don't believe a metaphorical novel has any right to exist until it exists on its ground floor. You know I never start with my characters as symbols. I'm unhappy if I can't see my characters. I mean, I not only have to know what they look like, and how tall they are, whether they're good looking or plain, but I also like to have some idea of what they smell like. . . .

INT.: . . . the kinds of experiences Rojack has, the vision of shooting arrows into Cherry's womb while she's singing in the night club, for example, seem to me to exist in a *dream* allegory but not at the literal level.

MAILER: I would disagree. I'd had the experience of being in night clubs and thinking evil thoughts and really barbing them like darts and sending them to people and seeing them react. At the time I didn't know whether I was profoundly drunk, or, you know, was I all alone in the world? But I had to recognize that there was a psychic reality to it. It wasn't just a phantasy. Since then there's been . . . so much material . . . to indicate that this is not at all unreasonable. For one thing, we do have telepathic powers, we talk about the human aura [as photographed in the Soviet Union through the Kirlian process], about the ability to send hostile vibrations, everybody uses that phrase, but, you know, if you can send a hostile vibration, which is to say, a hostile *wave,* why not employ modern theories of light and say hate appears not only in the form of a wave but also as a *particle?* If you can do it with light, you can do it with hate. In other words, send a damned particle into someone . . . my point is that there wasn't a single phenomenon in that book that I considered dreamlike or fanciful or fantastical. To me, it was a *realistic* book, but a realistic book at that place where extraordinary things are happening. I believe the experience of extraordinary people in extraordinary situations is not like our ordinary experience at all [Frank Norris's "variations from the type of normal life"] . . . . My metaphors explain more phenomena to me than any theology I can adopt. [my italics]

C. S. Lewis wrote in *The Allegory of Love* that "symbolism is a mode of thought, but allegory is a mode of expression." He explains:

The allegorist leaves the given—his own passions—to talk of that which is confessedly less real, which is a fiction. The symbolist leaves the given to find that which is more real. To put the difference in another way, for the symbolist it is we who are the allegory.

So, if it is the clockwork universe which is the allegory, then, perhaps, Lévi-Strauss's conclusion is correct after all: "Social life verifies the cosmology by its similarity of structure." Which is to say, as Lewis implies and Mailer testifies, the visionary writer scorns symbolism for its own sake, as the mere facilitation of verbal expression (in *Moby-Dick* Melville implies a similar distinction between allegory "hideous and disgusting" and analogy "O Nature, and O soul of man! how far beyond all utterance are your linked analogies!"). No "dream allegory" for Mailer, but Mailer will exalt the events of waking reality that his dreams tell him reflect most vividly the pervading structure of the whole. For example, in *Cannibals and Christians* Mailer has criticized John Updike because "like many a good writer before him, [he] does not know exactly what to do when action lapses, and so he cultivates his private vice, he *writes*." He offers an example from *Rabbit, Run* (which he labels *"True Confessions"*): "Outside in the air his fears condense. Globes of ether, pure nervousness, slide down his legs." Mailer's choice of this particular figure to criticize is confusing since it seems so similar to Mailer's own metaphors in its seemingly metaphysical equation of fear with sweat. Except that Updike as "implied author" clearly does not believe any such thing; this is just a clever, allegorical way of saying that a man sweats a lot when he is afraid, the conceit serving to camouflage the banality of the observation. But for Mailer, who is aware that science now has the capacity to heal the Cartesian split between matter and mind, there is no such thing as "poetic license"; the reader is asked to consider seriously the scientific validity of his metaphors, even when they appear to be "mixed," as in the following description of the first round of the Ali-Foreman fight:

Each veered backward like similar magnetic poles repelling one another forcibly.... Again they moved through invisible reaches of attraction and repulsion, darting forward, sliding to the side, cocking their heads, each trying to strike an itch to panic in the other, two big men fast as pumas, charged as tigers—unseen sparks came off their moves.

Do men and tigers move through electromagnetic fields of force that intensify to such an extent in archetypal experiences of danger that even the dull human eye can see them? The dream says it is so, and the new science seems to verify it.

As we approach the zenith of the circle, the old dualisms of mimesis and expressionism, realism and romance, seem to be breaking down before the unifying vision of the whole.

4

TO STRIKE THE
INSULTING SUN

If Northrop Frye's "Theory of Modes" (the "First Essay" in *Anatomy of Criticism*), which incorporates his "myth of eternal return," is superimposed upon the history of American fiction, it reveals, I believe, that ours is essentially a "comic" vision in which the deepening of ironic contradictions over the last one hundred and more years signals the return to what Frye calls the "idyllic" tradition of the romance mode or the "Apollonian" tradition of "mythical comedy." Comic is opposed, Frye states in *Fables of Identity,* to tragic:

... if we look at the quest-myth as a pattern of imagery, we see the hero's quest first of all in terms of its fulfillment. This gives us our central pattern of archetypal images, the vision of innocence which sees the world in terms of total human intelligibility. It corresponds to, and is usually found in the form of, the vision of the unfallen world or heaven in religion. We may call it the comic vision of life, in contrast to the tragic vision, which sees the quest only in the form of its ordained cycle. . . . The world of this apotheosis thus begins to pull away from the rotary cycle of the quest in which all triumph is temporary.

The dominant rhythm of American fiction is the product of a vision of reality which fits the comic pattern, a vision which has as its cornerstone the scientific validation of the myth "of total human intelligibility," of a world which makes sense after its own nonhuman fashion but into which man-the-animal is somehow keyed; the apotheosis being the pulling away from a purely human, rational, social pattern of eternal frustration to an "integration" (Frye's term for the "theme of the comic") with the larger cycles of the universe in which purely human concerns count for nothing. As Melville says of Pip's "madness": "So man's insanity is heaven's sense; and wandering from all mortal reason, man comes *at last* to that celestial thought, which, to reason, is absurd and frantic; and weal or woe, feels then uncompromised, *indifferent* as his God" (my italics).

According to Frye's chronology, one mode has been dominant at different stages in the development of civilization. The "myth" at the threshold of civilization; the "romance" in the early formative stages; the "high mimetic" from the time of Homer until, perhaps, the late eighteenth century; the "low mimetic" from the beginnings of realism in the eighteenth century until, perhaps, the rise of naturalism and objectivism at the end of the nineteenth century. And the "ironic mode" would seem to have dominated fiction from the end of the nineteenth century until the present. Any of these modes can participate in either the tragic or the comic vision in any given work. I will discuss the differences in the modes as the need arises, but the focus will, of necessity, fall on the ironic phase.

In both tragic irony and comic irony, the motif of the *pharmakos,* or scapegoat, dominates, tragically if the story is told from the point of view of the victim and comically if the story is told from society's point of view. Frye never suggests why the motifs of the ironic mode blend so easily back into the mythic, but perhaps the answer is in Frye's observation in *Anatomy of Criticism* that the cause-and-effect relationship between the hero's character flaw and his fall, a motif which dominates high and low mimetic tragedy, no longer defines the tragic hero of the ironic mode, shifting the emphasis from the "social life" to the "cosmology":

Tragic irony, then, becomes simply the study of tragic isolation as such, and it thereby drops out the element of the special case, which in some degree is in all the other modes. Its hero does not necessarily have any tragic hamartia [high mimetic] or pathetic obsession [low mimetic]:

he is only somebody who gets isolated from society [as in all tragic modes]. Thus the central principle of tragic irony is that whatever exceptional happens to the hero should be causally out of line with his character. . . . The *pharmakos* is neither innocent nor guilty. He is innocent in the sense that what happens to him is far greater than anything he has done provokes. . . . He is guilty in the sense that he is a member of a guilty society, or living in a world where such injustices are an inescapable part of existence.

The acausal principle seems also to be the primary factor in the progression of ironic comedy from naiveté along a downward plane of deepening ironic complexity (this is not a progression that takes place in time so much as in variations in the sophistication of the author and the audience). What is commonly called "melodrama," as in the detective story, the Western, or the thriller, "brings us to the figure of the scapegoat ritual and nightmare dream, the human symbol that concentrates our fears and hates." In the naive stage of the progression, the hero, who represents "the triumph of moral virtue over villainy, and the consequent idealizing of the moral views assumed to be held by the audience," locates and destroys or isolates the scapegoat, whose "villainy" represents an external threat to the established moral order. But there is always present in our psychological makeup, Frye seems to be suggesting, a sense of the "absurdity" of identifying "the enemy of society as a person outside that society," a psychological predisposition which seems the comic counterpart of the recognition that the punishment of the tragic ironic hero is "causally out of line" with what he is or has done. And this recognition in comedic forms "develops" in a four-stage progression "toward the opposite pole, which is true comic irony or satire, and which defines the enemy of society as a spirit within that society." For the sophisticated author and his sophisticated readers, the irony behind the confusion of cause-and-effect, the confusion over who is the victim and who the victimizer, deepens until

finally comes the comedy of manners, the portrayal of a chattering-monkey society devoted to snobbery and slander. In this kind of irony the characters who are opposed to or excluded from the fictional society have the sympathy of the audience [the audience and these characters are in "collusion," in Booth's terminology]. Here we are close to a parody of tragic irony, as we can see in the appalling fate of the relatively harmless hero of Evelyn Waugh's *A Handful of Dust.* Or we may have a character who, with the sympathy of the author or audience, repudiates such a society to the point of deliberately walking out of it, becoming thereby a kind of *pharmakos* in reverse. . . . It is more usual, however, for the artist to present an ironic deadlock in which the hero is regarded as a fool or worse by the fictional society, and yet impresses the real audience as having something more valuable than his society has. The obvious example, and certainly one of the greatest, is Dostoievsky's *The Idiot.* . . .

A comparison of two equally brilliant "chattering-monkey" stories, Aldous Huxley's "The Gioconda Smile" and Mark Twain's chapters 21 and 22 of *The Adventures of Huckleberry Finn,* reveals not only the particulars of the phenomenon but also how, in their particulars, English and American fiction differ. This takes us to Richard Chase's observation in *The American Novel and Its Tradition* on how the American novel is really a "romance" which has "approximated the poetry of idyl and of melodrama," and how it differs from the more purely "social" concerns of the more "realistic" English novel.

Mr. Hutton, the "hero" of Huxley's story, is a snob and a cad, personifying the quintessence of his upper class society's values, a man whose deepest emotion is the delight he feels because he can play the "heartless, amusing game" of social thrust-and-parry so well. As for the social pleasures of the Arkansas frontier villagers, "There couldn't anything wake them up all over, and make them happy all over, like a dog-fight— unless it might be putting turpentine on a stray dog and setting fire to him, or tying a tin pan to his tail and see him run himself to death." Two different but equally rotten societies.

Mr. Hutton, though innocent of the crime, becomes the scapegoat of his society when gossip convicts him of poisoning his wife in order to marry a "trollop." The irony is compounded by the fact that society could not have chosen a less appropriate scapegoat, Mr. Hutton being as incapable of committing the second offense (the more heinous of the two) as he is the first. As he tells the woman he supposedly murdered for,

"You seem to take it for granted that I murdered my wife. . . . It's really too grotesque. What do you take me for? A cinema hero? . . . Haven't you any conception of a civilized man's mentality? Do I look the sort of man who'd go about slaughtering people? I suppose you imagined that I was so insanely in love with you that I could commit any folly. When will you women learn that one isn't insanely in love?"

The irony is compounded further when we learn that Miss Spence, who has committed both crimes (she murdered Mrs. Hutton because of her passion for Mr. Hutton), is welcomed back into the society while the innocent victim is being driven out. Huxley has taken the standard narrative structure of high and low mimetic comedy, which involves a hero or heroine, dangerously close to being driven from society, being reintegrated with that society; and he has made the confusion of identities which is the stuff of such comedy reflect back on the appalling confusion of values that society inflicts on us. So, our sympathies, which had been with Miss Spence when we felt her to be the innocent victim of Mr. Hutton's snobbish cruelties, shift to Mr. Hutton when we realize that, just as Miss Spence is retreating into the defense mechanisms ("reaction formation," specifically) of the socially proper woman, Mr. Hutton is learning to feel.

The melodramatic spirit of the American story is more open, just as the sins of its society are more obvious. Old Boggs, the town drunk, has until one o'clock to stop insulting Colonel Sherburn in public. When he cannot bring himself to quit in time, Sherburn shoots him down in cold blood. By the values of the society Boggs is harmless, but his swaggering "blackguarding" is an affront to Sherburn's personal code of honor. Boggs becomes a scapegoat to Sherburn, a pasteboard mask behind which squats the petty maliciousness of his society. But Boggs's death is truly pathetic and moving because he is also just a dumb brute, who has a daughter who loves him and just happens to get the demon in him when he is drunk. He is the typical tragic ironic scapegoat because "he is innocent in the sense that what happens to him is far greater than anything he has done provokes. He is guilty in the sense that he is a member of a guilty society." Frye has written that in naive melodrama we come close to "the pure self-righteousness of the lynching mob." And if the reader is inclined to overvalue Boggs's role as a dumb brute, while refusing to recognize the artistic purpose in making him a pasteboard mask, the reader may misidentify this comedy as a tragedy and his sympathy may ride with the mob that forms to hang Sherburn. But Sherburn, the typical reverse-*pharmakos,* stops the mob, while repudiating their mindless, cowardly, sentimental society:

"The idea of *you* lynching anybody! It's amusing. The idea of you thinking you had pluck enough to lynch a *man!* Because you're brave enough to tar and feather poor friendless cast-out women that come along here, did that make you think you had grit enough to lay your hands on a *man?* Why, a *man's* safe in the hands of ten thousand of your kind—as long as it's daytime and you're not behind him. . . . Now the thing for *you* to do is to droop your tails and go home and crawl in a hole. If any real lynching's to be done it will be done in the dark, Southern fashion. . . ."

Huxley's story ends in "an ironic deadlock" with the hero possessed of "something more valuable than his society has," but with nowhere to go with it. Sherburn, on the other hand, can afford to deal boldly, defiantly with his society because he has the same option open to him that has been open to every American fictional hero from Natty Bumppo to Huck Finn to Lewis Medlock. If civilization begins to threaten him too severely, he can "light out for the territory." It is, perhaps, the vision of the "idyllic" which makes the melodramatic conflicts of our fiction so intense, which makes the heroes say "NO! in thunder" to their society. So, while "it is more usual" for the modern ironic comedy to end in "an ironic deadlock," our comic vision presents the saga of the "*pharmakos* in reverse." For Ahab, Rojack, the invisible man, D. J., and Lewis Medlock, defiance to the point of murder is the necessary first step in the process of "reintegration" with the natural order. This is what, for example, Ernest Hemingway's Robert Jordan achieves at the conclusion of *For Whom the Bell Tolls.* Despite the fact that he has failed to murder his scapegoat, Pablo, he achieves what no "cause" could give him:

He was completely *integrated* now and he took a good long look at everything. Then he looked up at the sky. There were big white clouds in it. He touched the palm of his hand against the pine needles where he lay and he touched the bark of the pine trunk that he lay behind. [my italics]

A vision of the end as the beginning which sounds very much like the epitaph that James Dickey told *Playboy* he has written for himself:

I want to be buried on the west bank of the Chattooga River. . . . Just dumped into a hole with no coffin. On a plain tombstone there'll be this: James Dickey, 1923 to 19 Whatever, American Poet And Novelist, Here Seeks His Deliverance.

Rejection by the chattering-monkey society appears to be the necessary prelude to "incorporation" into "a society of gods," which is, according to Frye, the mythic zenith of the historical cycle of comic fictional modes. This "theme of acceptance" takes the form in Christian literature of "the theme of salvation" or "assumption." That this is where our fiction is going is seen most clearly in Frye's description of the dominant motifs of romantic comedy, which stands right next to myth on the circle:

The mode of romantic comedy corresponding to the elegiac [Frye's descriptive term for romantic tragedy] is best described as idyllic, and its chief vehicle is the pastoral. . . . It preserves the theme of *escape from society* to the extent of idealizing a simplified life in the country or on the *frontier* (the pastoral of popular modern literature is the Western story). The close association with animal and vegetable nature that we noted in the elegiac recurs in the sheep and pleasant pastures (or the cattle and ranches) of the idyllic, and the same easy connection with myth recurs in the fact that such imagery is often used, as it is in the Bible, for the theme of *salvation*. [my italics]

The reverse-*pharmakos* hero is a permanent fixture in our fiction because, perhaps, there is something about the experience of the "idyllic" in "the presence of this continent" that brings us, as Fitzgerald put it, "face to face for the last time in history with something commensurate to" our "capacity for wonder," a wonder in the presence of what Richard Poirier calls "those moments where more is happening than one can easily assimilate," a wonder at the depths of our civilized minds that keeps our heroes beating on "ceaselessly into the past," back behind the pasteboard masks to the reality within.

Nineteenth-century science and especially biological determinism, Charles Child Walcutt implies in his influential book *American Literary Naturalism: A Divided Stream,* disrupted the "capacity for wonder" in the presence of the pastoral that seems, if we can believe the testimony of Emerson, Thoreau, and Whitman, our American literary heritage, dividing the mainstream of American "transcendental" idealism into two divergent streams. The great project of twentieth-century American novelists, Walcutt suggests, is a reconciliation of the two approaches:

My thesis is that naturalism is the offspring of transcendentalism. American transcendentalism asserts the unity of Spirit and Nature and affirms that intuition (by which the mind discovers its affiliation with Spirit) and scientific investigation (by which it masters Nature, the symbol of spirit) are equally rewarding and valid approaches to reality. When this mainstream of transcendentalism divides, as it does toward the end of the nineteenth century, it produces two rivers of thought. One, the approach to Spirit through intuition, nourishes idealism, progressivism, and social radicalism. The other, the approach to Nature through science, plunges into the dark canyon of mechanistic determinism. The one is rebellious; the other pessimistic; the one ardent, the other fatal; the one acknowledges will, the other denies it.

The split, as I read Walcutt, is not so much between the different approaches taken by different writers (as, for example, the difference between the rebelliousness of Jack London's protagonists and the pessimism of Theodore Dreiser) as it is a schizophrenic split in the approach of any given writer (as in what one might call the ardent fatalism of Ernest Hemingway). I maintain that the split has been healed to a great extent by the rise of the new science, that the "unity of Spirit and Nature" is being accomplished from the side of nature, that one could replace the term "intuition" with the term "instinct" and the term "Spirit" with something like the "unconscious" or the "confluent," acausal ordering principle. Such a theme appears in recent books like Thomas Berger's *Little Big Man,* Walker Percy's *Love in the Ruins,* Robert M. Pirsig's *Zen and the Art of Motorcycle Maintenance,* and Saul Bellow's *Humboldt's Gift,* but can be seen most clearly in the 1974 novel by Thomas McGuane, *Ninety-two in the Shade,* in which Thomas Skelton, a marine biologist by scientific training, returns by instinct to a simple life of guiding for sport fishermen on the open sea. His scientific training serving to make him a better guide, the daily battle of instinctual imperatives between him and the fish serving to make him a better scientist, and the combination serving to make him whole:

Thomas Skelton felt that simple survival at one level and the prevention of psychotic lesions based upon empirical observations of the republic depended upon his being able to get out on the ocean. Solitary floating as the tide carried him off the seaward shelf was in one sense sociopathic conduct for him; not infrequently such simplicity was one of three options; the others being berserking and smoking dope all the livelong day.

The merging of Thoreau's doctrine of simplification with the notion of sociopathy suggests again the basic antagonism between the society and the "isolate agonist." And it suggests that, perhaps, the plunge into "mechanistic determinism" that so unbalanced our early naturalistic writers and retarded the merging of the old with the new science was to a great extent inspired by social inhibitions and values. For example, in Emile Zola's *Germinal* (1885) the young boy Jeanlin is reduced by the poverty of the miners' strike to living in a cave like an animal, which engages the sympathy of the protagonist, Etienne. But when Jeanlin begins acting like an animal, Etienne reacts "with horror." In the scene in which Jeanlin murders a soldier, the animalism of his deed is evoked in such a way as to suggest the tragedy of a human being forced by environmental pressures to revert to instinctual behavior: "Jeanlin pulled himself up and crawled along on his hands, his thin spine arched like a cat's. His big ears, green eyes, and prominent jaws were quivering and ablaze with the excitement of his evil deed." But by the time of McGuane, the naturalistic writer's sympathies seem to have shifted from human values to those

of the natural order, and with the shift comes the image of the
human being, and not the animal, as inspiring disgust:

> His feeling of hope for a successful first-day guiding was considerably
> modified by Rudleigh's largely undeserved hooking of the fish. And now
> the nobility of the fish's fight was further eroding Skelton's pleasure.
> When they crossed the edge of the flat, the permit raced down the
> reef line in sharp powerful curves. . . . "Gawd, gawd, gawd," Rudleigh
> said. "This cookie is stronger than I am!" . . . A fish that was exactly
> noble, thought Skelton, who began to imagine the permit coming out
> of a deep-water wreck by the pull of moon and tide, riding the invisible
> crest of the incoming water, feeding and moving by force of blood;
> only to run afoul of an asshole from Connecticut.

The tension between melodrama and idyl that Chase observed operating in our fiction signals the passing of our fiction
from the melodramatic form of the ironic comedy to the idyllic
form of the romantic comedy, a project which was retarded
somewhat by the moral pessimism that early naturalistic writers
felt duty-bound to attach to biological determinism. The best
example is Frank Norris's *McTeague* (1899), a book balanced
tenuously between rebelliousness and pessimism, instinct and
morality, coming down awkwardly at the end on the side of
pessimism and the social good.

McTeague is a dumb brute: a huge, simple bear of a man who
somehow has become a dentist. He marries a sweet young girl,
Trina, who wins $5,000 in a lottery and soon becomes
psychotic in her miserly obsession. She reduces both of them
to poverty-stricken degradation after Marcus, a jealous suitor,
informs the state of California that McTeague has no diploma.
McTeague beats Trina to death after she refused to give him
the money, and he lights out for the territory out of which he
has originally come, but Marcus catches up with him in Death
Valley. McTeague kills Marcus but winds up handcuffed to the
dead body with nothing left to do but await his ironic fate.

Walcutt observes that there is something wrong with Norris's
grasp of cause-and-effect, that "the structure of the novel . . .
depends neither upon a 'cycle of degeneration' in which internal
forces direct the movement, nor upon a cycle of change induced

by external pressures operating in their regular courses." Norris must rely on an "adventure or intrigue" plot because, Walcutt suggests, his naturalistic philosophy has split into two streams:

He exhibits religious feeling which seems not to be related to his inchoate materialism. So shadowy are the philosophical assumptions, indeed, that he can endow McTeague with a sharp power of intuition through which, in the long final section devoted to his flight into the mountains and across the desert, he is constantly aware of his pursuers and knows when he must thrust on further into the hinterland. The suggestion is that this power of instinctive perception belongs to the atavistic animal nature which is strong in him. It is also a preview of the natural dynamism which derives from the romantic roots of naturalism and of which we shall see much more in *The Octopus* and *The Pit*.

This is an important analysis, but there are confusions. Walcutt concludes by explaining that though the novel "ends in outlandish melodrama rather than a controlled demonstration of inevitable consequences, it is merely because Norris shifted from the theory to the romantic extremes of naturalism." Yes, but why? And what are the romantic extremes?

McTeague's atavistic instincts awaken so dramatically and with such extrasensory power that McTeague in the wilderness is as superior to other men as McTeague in civilization is a hulking, slow-witted fool. The hero of the ironic mode, "inferior in power or intelligence to ourselves" and the victim of social "bondage, frustration or absurdity," has become the hero of either myth or romance, "superior" to other men in either "kind" or "degree," if we apply Frye's system to the novel. There is nothing "shadowy" about it: Norris saw clearly, through mists of pessimistic determinism, that this was not to be the story of a "cycle of degeneration" but the chattering-monkey story of McTeague's escape from the civilization which imprisons him. Thus, the nature of the plot is of necessity melodramatic rather than deterministic, for this is the story of the fight to regain the idyllic bond with nature. Walcutt states that nature is "malignant toward McTeague," but clearly it is society, not nature, which seeks McTeague's downfall. It is the following of society's imperatives and not instinct which leads to a tragic fall. It was the greed of Trina and Marcus that drove him from society, and it is the awakening of this corruption in him that is the only real danger he faces in the wilderness:

It was warning him again, that strange sixth sense, that obscure brute instinct. It was aroused again and clamoring to be obeyed. Here, in these desolate barren hills, twenty miles from the nearest human being, it stirred and woke and roweled him to be moving on. It had goaded him to flight from the Big Dipper mine, and he had obeyed. But now it was different; now he had suddenly become rich; he had lighted on a treasure. . . . How was he to leave that?

But he does leave it; his instincts save him from human corruption, and he is gone, beyond the grasp of any human power. And Norris knows he is free, but he cannot bring himself to accept the moral of his story; he cannot let McTeague get away with murder, not even the murder of Moby Dick. So he drops Marcus into the desert as a deus ex machina, and for good measure he traps McTeague among the least convincing group of symbols ever superimposed upon a bad ending: a pair of handcuffs, an empty desert, and a dead bird in a gilded cage.

We get a dramatic picture of where our fiction is going when we contrast this novel with Norman Mailer's use of the same plot sixty-six years later in *An American Dream*. Both McTeague's wife Trina and Rojack's wife Deborah function as scapegoats, pasteboard masks representing the corruptions of their societies, as opposed, for example, to Roberta in Dreiser's *An American Tragedy* who seems nothing more than a dumb-brute victim of fate. The injunction in *Moby-Dick* is to "strike *through*," not *at*, "the mask," and that is what both McTeague and Rojack do, murder becoming for both the gateway to salvation. And both Rojack and McTeague, driven from society by a posse in McTeague's case and two intense big-city detectives (teamed, ironically, with the Mafia) in Rojack's case, become scapegoats in reverse, rejecting social corruption for the pursuit of instinctual imperatives and reintegration with the natural order.

If the melodrama of *McTeague* becomes "outlandish," therefore, it is actually because Norris was unable to accept, with Mailer's vigor, "the romantic extremes of naturalism." The full implications of which, Mailer suggests in *An American Dream,* lead to "madness." But the alternative is a social sickness of which "cancer" is the physical expression. "Cancer," says Rojack, "is the growth of madness denied." So, Rojack, who has "lain with madness," has had a vision of heaven at the gateway of murder, and has talked with Graves's "moon-goddess," escapes into the Nevada desert, the same desert, ironically, in which McTeague's bones lie bleaching in the sun. And from the desert he makes his way through fields of electromagnetic force to the jungles of "Guatemala and Yucatán," back into the heart of darkness, there to seek his deliverance.

PART TWO

BUOYED UP BY THAT COFFIN

5

MELVILLE'S MAD MESSIAH

Richard Chase, in *The American Novel and Its Tradition,* identifies *Moby-Dick* as an American tragedy:

Undoubtedly the first step toward understanding *Moby-Dick* is to observe what is really very obvious: it is a book about the alienation from life that results from an excessive or neurotic self-dependence. . . . As Newton Arvin demonstrates, there is some reason to think of Ahab as guilty of *hybris,* in the Greek sense, or of excessive pride, in the Christian sense; but there is more reason to think of him as guilty or victimized by a distorted "self-reliance" [in Emerson's sense].

His perception of *Moby-Dick* as much like a classic or Christian tragedy is rather startling because he had previously assured us, in his introduction, that such works do not exist in the mainstream of our fiction:

The English novel . . . follows the tendency of tragic art and Christian art, which characteristically move through contradictions to forms of harmony, reconciliation, catharsis, and transfiguration.

Judging by our greatest novels, the American imagination, even when it wishes to assuage and reconcile the contradictions of life, has not been stirred by the possibility of catharsis or incarnation, by the tragic or Christian possibility. It has been stirred, rather, by the aesthetic possibilities of radical forms of alienation, contradiction, and disorder.

All parenthetical pagination in this chapter refers to the Norton Critical Edition of *Moby-Dick,* ed. Harrison Hayford and Hershel Parker (New York: 1967).

Rather than an interpretation of *Moby-Dick* as an "epic-romance" as he had promised, Chase joins Arvin, Matthiessen, Charles Olson, and just about everyone else in emphasizing the tragic flaw in Ahab's character and, thus, the tragic misdirection of Ahab's quest. But the theme does not necessarily have to be: one man's madness imposed on the universe; it could be more like: the madness of the universe imposed on one man. Matthiessen suggests as much in *American Renaissance:* "Hawthorne was concerned with depicting the good and evil within man's heart. Melville is not so concerned with individual sin as with titanic uncontrollable forces which seem to dwarf man altogether." Against these forces Ahab strives, like Prometheus defying Zeus, Odysseus struggling against Poseidon, and that is heroic, epic, even mythic, because Ahab's quest is larger than his own obsession; Ahab strives for all men because his misfortune has taught him, as Ishmael puts it, that "all men"

live enveloped in whale lines. All men are born with halters round their necks; but it is only when caught in the swift, sudden turn of death, that mortals realize the silent, subtle, ever-present perils of life. And if you be a philosopher, though seated in the whale-boat, you would not at heart feel one whit more of terror, than though seated before your evening fire with a poker, and not a harpoon, by your side. (241)

It is not, I would argue, the tragic vision but the comic vision of "total human intelligibility" that is at the core of the book. To see this we have to start with Leslie Fielder's observation in *Love and Death in the American Novel* that Ahab and Ishmael are "two halves of a single epic," not tragic, "hero." Ishmael carries on for Ahab as Peter carried on for Jesus or Joshua for Moses to achieve the final "apotheosis" (in Frye's terminology) that has been made possible by, but ultimately, denied to, Ahab. In fact, Ralph Ellison, as he has stated in John O'Brien's *Interviews with Black Writers,* sees this comic pattern of "redemption" not only in *Moby-Dick* but also in the mainstream of American literature and even the whole of Western literature:

INTERVIEWER: ... the hero in most American novels, and perhaps even in most Western literature, ends in either alienation or death.

ELLISON: I don't think that I can go along with your analysis. Oedipus is defeated and Christ is defeated; they're both defeated in one sense, and yet they live. Raskolnikov is defeated; he's found out and sent to Siberia. But there's a promise of *redemption*. ... You've got an ambiguous movement from defeat to *transcendence* in those works. Ahab is defeated but Ishmael isn't. Ishmael brings back the story and the lesson; he's gone to the underworld and has returned. Gatsby ends up dead but the narrator does not; he gives us the account. ... You have these ambiguous defeats and survivals which constitute the pattern of all literature. The reason for that is that literature is an affirmative act. ... Underlying it most profoundly is the sense that man dies but his values continue. The mediating role of literature is to leave the successors with the sense of what is dangerous in the human predicament and what is glorious. That's why we must judge literature, not on the basis of its thematic content or its technical innovations, but on its *vision* of the human condition. [my italics]

Critics may become confused by the American innovation on the classic comic pattern of having a dramatized narrator take over for the fallen hero, a device used not only in *Moby-Dick* and *The Great Gatsby* but also in *Deliverance* and Ken Kesey's *One Flew over the Cuckoo's Nest* (1962). But there is another source of confusion. In his "Theory of Modes" Frye suggests that at least one form of low mimetic tragedy bears a close resemblance to comedy. In low mimetic tragedy the hero is often an *alazon,* the miles gloriosus of comedy who "pretends or tries to be something more than he is," the pretension in tragedy taking the form of "a mania or obsession." Conrad's Lord Jim is such a low mimetic tragic hero, according to Frye, who concludes with this observation:

It is, of course, quite possible to take the *alazon* at his own valuation: this is done for instance by the creators of the inscrutable gloomy heroes in Gothic thrillers, with their wild or piercing eyes and their dark hints of interesting sins. The result as a rule is not tragedy so much as the kind of melodrama which may be defined as comedy without humor. When it rises out of this, we have a study of obsession presented in terms of fear instead of pity: that is, the obsession takes the form of an unconditioned will that drives its victim beyond the normal limits of humanity.

This description fits Ahab and *Moby-Dick* so well that it appears we have no problem. However, as I have suggested (pp. 43, 51), there is a connection between the immersion in "the destructive element" and the comic vision which militates against the tragic interpretation of both *Lord Jim* and *Moby-Dick*. It may be too that both works are a little farther along on the modal circle than traditional interpretations would lead us to believe; it may be that we have in *Moby-Dick* not the melodrama of the low mimetic tragic Gothic but the melodrama of the ironic comic, chattering-monkey mode; it may be, in fact, that all the works studied here have passed beyond the ironic nadir and are well along on the ascending phase of Frye's diachronic cycle. (I am intrigued by the possibility that on the dark, ascending phase there is a low romantic mode which precisely balances Frye's low mimetic and to which a work like *Moby-Dick* might belong; balancing the high mimetic would be the high romantic. In such a system myth and irony would not be modes, but the polar tendencies of what might be called the structure and texture phases, respectively, of the cycle. When the high romantic mode swings too far toward pure structure, it might be said to initiate the pathetic shift, and when the low mimetic mode swings too far toward structurelessness, it might be said to initiate the heroic shift.)

To so classify *Moby-Dick* it will be necessary to suggest just what it is that Ahab "repudiates" in his role as "half" a reverse-*pharmakos* and just what life-renewing vision is to be won from his act of defiance. Leo Marx, in his brilliant analysis of *Moby-Dick* in *The Machine in the Garden,* implies that a critic cannot reach such determinations by studying only the "literary consequences" of an author's vision but must move toward its "extra-literary causes," which, according to Marx, was for Melville a "complex" vision of the pastoral.

The theme of *Moby-Dick,* like that of *Lord Jim,* is "How to be!" Marx begins his study of Melville's approach to this question with a letter Melville wrote to Hawthorne in June 1851, in which he deprecates a very romantic-sounding quotation from Goethe, "Live in the all." Melville comments that "what plays mischief with the truth is that men insist upon the universal application of a temporary feeling or opinion." What Melville calls "this 'all' feeling" bears an uncomfortable resemblance to Emerson's famous sentence: "I am nothing; I see all; the currents of the Universal Being circulate through me; I am part or parcel of God." So, Marx seems justified in his conclusion that Melville is above all convinced that immersion in transcendental or romantic pastoralism is *not* "how to be":

... what enables him to write this astonishing letter is unsparing self-knowledge; he is exposing the basis of pastoral fantasying in himself, and his insight illuminates *Moby-Dick.* The final sentence [as quoted above] alone, which contains the gist of what Ishmael learns aboard the *Pequod,* neatly circumscribes the romantic pastoralism, always verging upon pantheism, of Goethe, Wordsworth, and Emerson. The extravagant claims of that doctrine, Melville is saying, stem from a tendency to confuse a transitory state of mind—the "all" feeling—with the universal condition of things. ... The letter is a treatise in small against excessive trust in what Freud calls the "oceanic feeling." With one clean, surgical stroke Melville severs the nineteenth century's burgeoning, transcendental metaphysic from its psychic roots.

The key words in the quotation above are "excessive trust," for it is not the pastoral vision that Melville would have Ahab repudiate but the "faith" a man maintains at the cost of his intellectual integrity. Starbuck's is such a faith, and his apostrophe to the sea, standing in contrast to Ishmael's earlier apostrophe to Bulkington and his "great, deep intellect," reveals to us that Starbuck does not know "how to be": "Loveliness unfathomable, as ever lover saw in his young bride's eye!— Tell me not of they teeth-tiered sharks, and thy kidnapping cannibal ways. Let faith oust fact; let fancy oust memory; I look deep down and do believe" (406).

Starbuck is providing one answer here to the central paradox that motivates Ahab's quest: the duality of nature. On one hand, according to Marx, there is "an idyllic domain, a lovely green land that figures a simple, harmonious accommodation to the conditions of nature," and, on the other hand, "hideous, menacing wilderness, habitat of cannibals and sharks located beyond (or hidden beneath the surface of) the bland green pastures." Ishmael's heroism, Marx implies, stems from his attempt to "reconcile the apparent contradiction between these two states of nature," but Starbuck's answer to the question of "how to be" in the face of such knowledge is simply to believe in the first and ignore the second, while Ahab has "forsaken the peaceful land, for forty years to make war on the horrors of the deep," refusing, for the sake of the quest, to give "but small entrance to any sympathy from the green country without" (443).

Henry A. Murray in his famous article "In Nomine Diaboli" has suggested that such a quest indicates that Ahab has "been possessed by" or "sold his soul to the Devil." But is this not, as Joseph Campbell has made clear in *The Hero with a Thousand Faces,* the same descent to the underworld that our heroes have always undertaken without being branded as demonic? While Marx declares that Melville "moves his narrator toward a saving resolution," he does not give full emphasis to the necessary connection between Ahab's perceptions and Ishmael's intellectual salvation. Ahab saves Ishmael from the horrors of "excessive" pantheism and in particular Emersonian transcendentalism, and it is Ishmael who returns from the underworld with what Campbell calls *"the power to bestow boons on his fellow man."*

Ishmael's first brush with this monster occurs in the famous section "The Mast-Head," in which Ishmael speculates on the fate of dreamy romantics like himself when they give their minds up to the "deep, blue, bottomless soul" they perceive to be "pervading mankind and nature" (140), only to have their "identity" come back too late to prevent a horrifying death fall. Marx:

What Melville is describing, of course, is a consummate Emersonian experience of nature. Natural facts are blended with Ishmael's thoughts by the rhythm of the sea, and so he merges with the all. . . . In Melville's case, however, the interlude does not lead to an affirmation of a transcendent meaning. On the contrary, "The Mast-Head" is designed to show that such *fantasies* may end in horror.

Melville's theme, which he had introduced at the very beginning of the book shortly after Ishmael's query, "Are the green fields gone?"— is that the romantic attitude toward nature is finally *narcissistic*. [my italics]

That last sentence is a reference to Ishmael's early observations on the myth of Narcissus, which, he says, "is the key to it all" (14). Sigmund Freud always understood that there is a duality operating in nature and in mankind, and in his early formulations, according to Norman O. Brown in *Life against Death,* he identified the two antagonists as the "sexual instinct working to preserve the species [the "pleasure-principle"] and the self-preservation instinct [the "reality-principle"] working to preserve the individual member of the species." However, as Freud came to develop his theory of narcissism, he realized that what he had thought of as a basic instinct, self-preservation, was really just a manifestation of the narcissistic process: the ego transferring love from its normal object such as the mother ("object-libido") to itself ("ego-libido"). Thus, the two turn out to be aspects of the same instinct, which Freud, in his later writings, came to call Eros, or the life instinct. And, taking a hint from biological science, he called its new antagonist Thanatos, or the death instinct. The one, according to Brown, seeking ever and ever greater unifications "to preserve and enrich life," and the other seeking to divide and disrupt these unities in order "to return life to the peace of death." But this in turn leads Freud to a new vision of the corruption inherent in narcissism, a vision which Melville seems to have shared. Freud, in *The Ego and the Id* (1923):

The transformation of erotic libido into ego-libido of course involves an abandonment of sexual aims, a desexualization. In any case this throws light upon an important function of the ego in its relation to Eros. By thus obtaining possession of the libido from the object-cathexes, setting itself up as sole love-object, and desexualizing or sublimating the libido of the id, the ego is working in opposition to the purposes of Eros and placing itself at the service of the opposing instinctual trends [the death instinct].

Narcissism blocks Eros by blocking union, and it blocks union (adult sexual activity) by replacing reality (an object-cathexis) with fantasy (what Brown calls an infantile "dream of narcissistic omnipotence"). Brown:

Fantasy is essentially regressive; it is not just a memory, but the hallucinatory reanimation of memory, a mode of self-delusion substituting the past for the present—or rather, by negation identifying past and present.... the pregenital and genital organizations are constituted by regressive fantasies of union with the mother, attached to the specific organs where the infantile drama of separation is enacted [the oral, the anal, and the phallic stages of developing sexuality]. For example, the prototype of all "transformation of object-libido into narcissistic libido," and therefore the prototype of all sublimation ..., is infantile thumb-sucking, in which, with the aid of a fantasy or dream of union with the mother, the child makes himself into both himself and his mother's breast [hence, a fantasy of union of Self and Other]. Altogether, therefore, the world of fantasy is that opaque shield with which the ego protects himself from reality and through which the ego sees reality; it is by living in a world of fantasy that we lead a desexualized life. In sublimation [of] the erotic component, what is projected is these infantile fantasies, not the reality of the id. Sublimation is the continuation not of infantile sexuality [the "polymorphously perverse"] but of infantile dreaming.

Ishmael exhibits these symptoms, according to Marx, in chapters such as "A Squeeze of the Hand," but from Ahab's example he will finally outgrow, as Marx puts it, "his proclivity to childish pleasure fantasies." Ahab's example will teach Ishmael, as Jim's taught Marlow, how to "Be True," (355, "that mortal man who hath more of joy than sorrow in him, that mortal man cannot be true"). It is clear, as Richard Chase has said in *The American Novel and its Tradition,* that *Moby-Dick* "is to offer the alternative to Narcissus."

But it is also clear that Chase is wrong when he says, "To be Ahab is to be unable to resist the hypnotic attraction of the self with its impulse to envelop and control the universe." Actually, to be Ahab is to be able to see beyond the reflected image of the self (narcissism) to the cosmic forces waiting to devour the dreamer as sharks wait to devour the water gazer. And Ishmael comes to share Ahab's insight that the individual, far from being "part or parcel" of the benign all, is infected with the same duality that infects nature. Looking into the water, Ishmael sees not the idyllic self but the idyllic self corrupted:

> Consider the subtleness of the sea; how its most dreaded creatures glide under water, unapparent for the most part, and treacherously hidden beneath the loveliest tints of azure. Consider also the devilish brilliance and beauty of many of its most remorseless tribes, as the dainty embellished shape of many species of sharks. Consider, once more, the universal cannibalism of the sea; all whose creatures prey upon each other, carrying on eternal war since the world began.
> Consider all this; and then turn to this green, gentle, and most docile earth; consider them both, the sea and the land; and do you not find a strange analogy to something in yourself? For as this appalling ocean surrounds the verdant land, so in the soul of man there lies one insular Tahiti, full of peace and joy, but encompassed by all the horrors of the half known life. God keep thee! Push not off from that isle, thou canst never return! [235-36]

Ishmael is of course being facetious in that advice, for he realizes, as Melville's Tommo did in *Typee,* that destruction lurks in that insular paradise, that one buys sanctuary from what Marx calls the "hideous wilderness" only at the price of one's personality, only on condition of a regression to what Marx calls "primitive mindlessness." In fact, when Freud and Brown connect infantile narcissistic fantasizing to the process of desexualization or sublimation, they are implicating society in the cosmic plot against the individual's struggle to achieve an independent, adult, reality-oriented personality. This is how Brown interprets Freud's "myth of the primal horde," which Freud saw as the prototype of all civilization:

> The essential point in the Freudian diagnosis of human sociability was seen by Roheim: men huddle into hordes as a substitute for parents, to save themselves from independence, from "being left alone in the dark." Society was not constructed, as Aristotle says, for the sake of life and more life, but from defect, from death and the flight from death, from fear of separation and fear of individuality. Thus Freud derives fear of "separation and expulsion from the horde" from castration anxiety, and castration anxiety from the fear of separation from the mother and

the fear of death. Hence there are no social groups without a religion of their own immortality, and history-making is always the quest for group-immortality.

Chase's description of Ahab's flaw actually describes the obsessions of the chattering-monkey society (12, "thousands upon thousands of mortal men fixed in ocean reveries"), which Ahab repudiates when he denies Starbuck's final plea for socially defined sanity in "The Symphony." Thus, Marx's interpretation fails only in not recognizing the repudiation, fails only in insisting on Ahab's tragic identity as "the perverted, monomaniac incarnation of the Age of Machinery." It is a curious lapse, since Marx seems to understand perfectly that Ahab's obsession with civilization's machinery is not a symptom of his monomaniacal "impulse to envelop and control" but of his awareness that society is the mirror of what he has found at the heart of the universe. For example, Marx keys on the image of the whale skeleton grown over with green vines in "A Bower in the Arsacides," an image which seems to acknowledge Schopenhauer's concept of will and to presage Thomas Hardy's concept of the Immanent Will and which may be the most implicit analogue in the book:

Through the lacings of the leaves, the great sun seemed a flying shuttle weaving the unwearied verdure.... Speak, weaver! ... Nay—the shuttle flies—the figures float from forth the loom; the freshet-rushing carpet for ever slides away. The weaver-god, he weaves; and by that weaving is he deafened, that he hears no mortal voice; and by that humming, we, too, who look on the loom are deafened.... For even so it is in all material factories. [374]

"It is," says Marx, "a bold conceit, this green factory inside the whale—another vivid metaphor of American experience; Ishmael deliberately making his way to the center of primal nature only to find, when he arrives, a premonitory sign of industrial power." Marx seems to have missed his own point; the American experience of the pastoral has taught that it is the age of machinery, not Ahab, that is "the perverted, monomaniac incarnation" of the cosmic mechanism of fate, the social life once again verifying the cosmology by its similarity of structure: as Ahab tells Starbuck, "By heaven, man, we are turned round and round in this world, like yonder windlass, and Fate is the handspike" (445). And it is this clairvoyance alone which saves Ahab (as McTeague's instincts will save him from the lure of greed) from being drawn back into the orbit of society's versions of pastoral:

"But it is a mild, mild wind, and a mild looking sky; and the air smells now, as if it blew from a far-away meadow; they have been making hay somewhere under the slopes of the Andes, Starbuck, and the mowers are sleeping among the new-mown hay. Sleeping? Aye, toil how we may, we all sleep at last on the field. Sleep? Aye, and *rust* amid greenness; as last year's scythes flung down, and left in the half-cut swaths—Starbuck!" [my italics]

The duality of nature and the antagonistic operation of the instincts suggest that there are only two ways "to be." Both Ishmael and Ahab conceptualize the antagonism in the same terms in which Freud would cast the life versus the death instinct: the passive feminine versus the aggressive masculine (235, 262, 375, 412, 417, 442). Ishmael contrasts, for example the "woman's look" of the "pensive air" with "the robust and manlike sea," the "snow-white wings of small, unspeckled birds" that are "the gentle thoughts of the feminine air" (as in Swedenborg and Emerson) with the "mightly leviathans, sword-fish, and sharks" which are "the strong, troubled, murderous thinkings of the masculine sea" (442). If it could be this simple, then the tragic interpretation of Ahab's quest would be tenable: Ahab's dismemberment overburdens his ego with the "irremediable aggressiveness" (Marx's phrase) that leads him to deny the life-sustaining submissiveness of Starbuck. But in *Beyond the Pleasure Principle* (1920) Freud postulated that the interaction of the instincts is not that simple. The riddle of narcissism and the phenomena of masochism and sadism suggested to Freud that aggression can serve Eros as narcissism can serve Thanatos:

How is one to derive the sadistic impulse, which aims at the injury of the object, from the life-sustaining Eros? Does not the assumption suggest itself that this sadism is properly a death-instinct which is driven apart from the ego by the influence of the narcissistic libido, so that it becomes manifest only in reference to the object? It then enters the service of the sexual function. . . . It takes over, with the aim of propagation, the function of so far overpowering the sex-object as the carrying out of the sexual act demands. . . . Where the original sadism experiences no abatement or fusion, the well-known hate-love ambivalence of the love-life is set up.

The complete interaction and paradoxical interdependence of the life and death instincts were fully understood by Melville, as most brilliantly demonstrated in the image of the whale skeleton (the masculine principle of death) serving as a trellis for the green vines (the feminine principle of life):

Now, amid the green, life-restless loom of that Arsacidean wood, the great, white, worshipped skeleton lay lounging—a gigantic idler! Yet, as the ever-woven verdant warp and woof intermixed and hummed around him, the mighty idler seemed the cunning weaver; himself all woven over with the vines; every month assuming greener, fresher verdure; but himself a skeleton. Life folded Death; Death trellised Life; the grim god wived with youthful Life, and begat him curly-headed glories. [275]

Such a vision of the universe suggests that the reverse-*pharmakos* hero's passage from the assumptions of a sick society to godlike understanding of the whole will be determined to some extent by his capacity for "negative capability," his capacity for resting amid, balancing among, the contradictions, indeterminacies, and ironies that are the nature of nature. The answer to the fundamental question of "How to Be" seems to lie in the individual's ability to "strike the uneven balance" between the masculine and feminine approaches to existence. Ishmael does achieve this "saving resolution," according to Marx, but to appreciate fully the subtlety of Melville's vision, it will be necessary to examine still more closely the relation of mankind's unconscious instincts to the design of nature.

Nature, according to Freud in *Beyond the Pleasure Principle,* provides man's body with an external "barrier against stimuli" that enables man to deal effectively with the undifferentiated mass of external stimuli that bombard his "perceptual consciousness" system. This system lies "on the boundary between the outer and the inner," and so, unfortunately, it provides no protection from painful stimuli, "anxiety," which arise from within the unconscious. Thus, the individual will learn to "project" these stimuli to sources in the outside world "in order for it to be possible to apply against them the defensive measures of the barrier against stimuli." Freud had all along believed that the unconscious functioned according to the dictates of "the pleasure principle," but with *Beyond the Pleasure Principle* he began to theorize that there is a pleasure beyond pleasure, a pleasure in "the impulse to obtain mastery of a situation," and so he was moved to postulate a "repetition compulsion" as the ground of all instinctual behavior. A child in his play, Freud observed, is as apt to repeat a painful experience as a pleasurable one, and in such a re-enactment of pain the process of projection looms large: "In passing from the passivity of experience to the activity of play the child applies to his playfellow the unpleasant occurrence that befell himself and so *avenges* himself on the person of this *proxy*" (my italics).

Both Henry A. Murray and Newton Arvin see this same process behind Ahab's revenge quest, Murray calling Moby Dick the "projection of Captain Ahab's Presbyterian conscience" and Arvin in *Herman Melville* calling him the projection of the "archetypal parent" (the superego or conscience in Freud's thinking is, of course, the internalization of social and parental control). The question that is never confronted except obliquely is: what is Ahab seeking to master in seeking to murder Moby Dick? The concept of projection suggests that it is a part of himself, an anxiety deep within, that he would kill. Ahab says as much: "Oh! how valiantly I seek to drive out of others' hearts what's clinched so fast in mine!" (459). Ahab does not seek to abolish death, only the fear of death, and the fear of death in the human unconscious works through the imagistic process (introjection necessarily precedes projection). And, as Ernest Hemingway has observed in the introduction to *Men at War* (1942), "Cowardice, as distinguished from panic, is almost always simply a lack of ability to suspend the functioning of the imagination."

In his concept of "castration anxiety," Freud postulated that the child internalizes the parents' punishing power (the superego) through an image of physical castration, but in his later writings, as Norman O. Brown has made clear, he began to see castration anxiety as just the imagistic expression of all primal experiences of separation, from the birth trauma on:

> ... all these separations are experienced as a threat of death: again in Freud's own words, what the ego fears in anxiety "is in the nature of an overthrow or extinction." Thus Freud's own analysis shows, although Freud himself never said so, that there is a close and deep connection between anxiety and the death instinct. Anxiety is a response to experiences of separateness, individuality, and death. The human child, which at the mother's breast experiences a new and intense mode of union, of living, and of loving, must also experience a new and intenser mode of separation, individuality, and death.... In the human family the expansion of Eros onto a new and higher level entails the expansion of death onto a new and higher level. It is because the child loves the mother so much that it feels separation from the mother as death. As a result, birth and death, which at the biological level are experienced once only, are at the human psychic level experienced constantly; the child can say with St. Paul, "I die daily."

Freud postulated in his later writings a "Nirvana principle" underlying the pleasure principle, and he conceptualized it as the state of quiescence of inorganic matter to which the living organism compulsively seeks to return. At this point in Freud's thinking, according to Herbert Marcuse in *Eros and Civilization,* the early tendency to see the unconscious as a "monism of sexuality" threatens once again to undermine the dualistic conception through the identification of the pleasure principle (Eros) and the Nirvana principle (Thanatos), becoming a "monism of death." But Brown adds an important clarification to Freud's thought that keeps the dualism from collapsing: man suffers from a peculiar "instinctual ambivalence" because only man among the animals is on a "flight from death," and the flight is linked through the imagistic process to the primal separation anxiety. It would seem that Brown is postulating an adjunct to the Nirvana principle which I will call the Grim Reaper principle. Freud had linked anxiety to repression early in his career, but later on, Brown explains, he began to see that repression, rather than causing, is caused by this primal anxiety; all repression, then, is really the repression of the fear of death. The energy of these two principles, the Grim Reaper and Nirvana, is displaceable, so that both Eros and Thanatos can have the power both to push and to pull. A man may fear separation so much that he activates grim visions of, in Shakespeare's words, "woe, destruction, ruin, and decay," so that he is driven to seek reunification with a substitute for the mother in the sex act. Or a man may fear separation so much that he will be driven, in Brown's words, "to erotize death—to activate a morbid wish to die, a wish to regress to the prenatal state before life (and separation) began, to the mother's womb."

The important insight toward which Brown is moving is that the Grim Reaper and Nirvana, rather than representing Eros and Thanatos respectively, are two sides of the same coin, two sides of what Brown calls "the universal neurosis of mankind." The more inclusive principles of life and death will use them for their own purposes, but in the meantime mankind will be sick. The new dialectic which Brown sees emerging in man, although once again he does not give it so explicit a name, is the "fear of death" versus "the acceptance of death," the resolution of which will not overthrow life versus death but will cure the sickness to which only man, as the only animal with an imagination, is subjected. Both Brown and Marcuse emphasize that Freud maintained that the basic instincts of life and death are "fused" at the biological level, giving rise in their writings to a sense of optimism for a life-sustaining return of man's psyche to the natural, animal innocence from which it came: a comic vision of apotheosis that Brown calls "the resurrection of the body" and Marcuse "the liberation of Eros."

But first, says Brown, man must become "strong enough to die." The importance of this first step is easily seen, according to Brown, if we regard "the sexual organizations"—the oral, anal, and phallic fixations—as not just stages in sexual maturation but "the effect on the body of anxiety in the ego" (the imagination invests each organ with power over death; one fears the loss of that power). Thus, "the sexual organizations were perhaps constructed by the ego in its flight from death, and could be abolished by an ego strong enough to die," Brown declares. What will be abolished with the phallic fixation will be the Grim Reaper image of dismemberment, castration, and mutilation (the primordial power of which has been recently demonstrated by the unprecedented box office success of *Jaws*), and man's psyche will be at peace in a state of resolution that Brown sees as analogous to or a return to the state of infantile, preorganized, "polymorphously perverse" pleasure in "the active life of all the human body." Likewise, with the Grim Reaper image neutralized, there will no longer be a compulsive fixation on Nirvana and mindlessness. Ishmael will be able to enjoy the active delights of the Mast-Head without fearing for his life; likewise, he will be able to look as long as he wishes into "the face of the fire" without having to fear losing control of the tiller; Thoreau will know that he is free to move out of his cabin at the Pond, and Emerson will be able to work up the determination to move in. The believers, to put the issue in Melville's terms, will no longer fear to put off their "coloring glasses" and the unbelievers will no longer go blind gazing at "the monumental white shroud" (170).

Moby Dick has "reaped away Ahab's leg with his sickle-shaped lower jaw, as a mower a blade of grass in the field" (160) and so become the Grim Reaper, "the monomaniac incarnation of all those malignant agencies which some deep men feel eating in them, till they are left living on with half a heart and half a lung." And, thus, the imagination's fear of mutilation, seemingly beyond neutralization or ameliorization, is "made practically assailable" in the projection that is Moby Dick. Harmony, resolution, psychic wholeness are suddenly within striking distance, with the hope that by striking at the projection a blow will also "strike through" to the source of the fear that so cripples the human intellect.

Before proceeding to an analysis of the apotheosis toward which Ahab's religion of defiance is leading, it will be necessary to make a case for Ahab's messianic powers of clairvoyance, for, if his projection of hate onto Moby Dick is solely unconscious, then he may be justly labeled psychotic (pp. 19-20). The key to his strange powers, as Ishmael points out, is that, as his madness grew, "not one jot of his great natural intellect had perished" (161). He is never in danger, therefore, of confusing Moby Dick, the dumb brute, with the Grim Reaper image he has become: "I see in him outrageous strength, with an inscrutable malice sinewing it. That inscrutable thing is chiefly what I hate; and be the white whale agent, or be the white whale principal, I will wreak that hate upon him" (145). Ishmael, who is beginning to absorb many of Ahab's powers of clairvoyance, solidifies the rightness of Ahab's concept of projection with an observation that seems to imply that there is a connection between the Self and the Other, the inner "drive" and its external aim, between the projector and the projection, that is too implicit to be mere coincidence:

Ah, ye admonitions and warnings! why stay ye not when ye come? But rather are ye predictions than warnings, ye shadows! Yet not so much predictions from without, as verifications of the foregoing things within. For with little external to constrain us, the innermost necessities in our being, these still drive us on. [145]

The most spectacular psychological event in *Moby-Dick* is Ahab's vision of the "clear spirit of clear fire," "fiery father" of the universe, in "The Candles." Projecting the castration complex onto the universe, he sees that the "sweet mother" personifies the "queenly personality" that confers on the human animal not just life but life more abundantly, which is the human equivalent of the "low, enjoying power" (147) shared by all animals. Ishmael shares this half of Ahab's vision: "Man must eventually lower . . . his conceit of attainable felicity; not placing it anywhere in the intellect or the fancy; but in the wife, the heart, the bed, the table, the saddle, the fireside, the country" (349). But Ahab also sees a masculine, castrating father who has separated the human being from the mother principle ("Oh, cruel! what hast thou done with her?"), from the pastoral element that surrounds him ("damned in the midst of Paradise").

The great project of human life, its "puzzle," is to learn how to love the mother in the presence of the menacing father. The great insight of Ahab is that the worship of the mother, which involves "love" and "reverence," necessitates the "right worship" of the father, which is "defiance," because to "neither love nor reverence" will the father "be kind" (417). To return to the Oedipus myth for a moment (p. 38), a man is, after all, born from two, and he invites tragedy when he either fears the father so much that he denies the father's power to separate him from the mother (religion) or fears the father so much that he "identifies" (Freud's term) with the father's ruthless aggressiveness and denies the biological dependence on the mother (culture). To take the second first, Ahab has sensed Brown's dictum that society is an elaborate construct erected to fight the "fear of separation" (p. 69). While "animals let death be a part of life, and use the death instinct to die," Brown declares, "man aggressively builds immortal cultures and makes history in order to fight death." The irony is, as Freud made clear in *Moses and Monotheism* (1939) with his "myth of the primal horde," society must perpetuate the fear of death to insure its own immortality, must keep alive the memory of the castrating father (totemism) through the manufacture of a "patriarchal God" and enforce "a renunciation of instinctual gratification" through the ruthless mechanisms of the "paternalistic state." If, as Murray maintains, Moby Dick is the projection of Ahab's "Presbyterian conscience," and that conscience is the image of the Grim Reaper, this is why it needs to be mastered. Likewise, to identify too strongly with the mother is not to love the mother but, in Brown's words, to "erotize death." Fear of the Grim Reaper image leads not to love of the mother's image but to an obsession with Nirvana, an "I-am-nothing" mentality that Melville saw infecting the transcendentalism of Emerson.

One can love the mother, then, only by defying the fear of death. To defy is not to deny; it is to recognize death's "unconditional, unintegral mastery" (417), to recognize with Freud in *The Ego and the Id* that life is, finally, nothing but "a continuous descent towards death" and still to affirm the "one insular Tahiti" within. Ahab would "strike the uneven balance" that will restore to man the possibility of a qualified return to the pastoral condition, the "society of gods," and the balance struck, as Ishmael discovers, is two-to-one in favor of masculine "sorrow" over feminine "joy" (355). Ahab, as a "Man of Sorrows," is the "truest of all men," but ultimately he cannot accept the odds, identifies too strongly with the need for defiance;

and so Ahab, given one last chance to strike his own balance
in "The Symphony," rejects what Marx describes as the "saving
resolution" of Ishmael, who has followed Ahab into "woe"
to the brink of "madness" but not beyond. Ishmael, "buoyed
up by that coffin" (470), discovers the secret of "How to be":

There is a wisdom that is woe; but there is a woe that is madness. And
there is a Catskill eagle in some souls that can alike dive down into the
blackest gorges, and soar out of them again and become invisible in the
sunny spaces. And even if he for ever flies within the gorge, that gorge
is in the mountains; so that even in his lowest swoop the mountain eagle
is still higher than other birds upon the plain, even though they soar. [355]

But against the image of Ishmael as a sad eagle soaring,
Melville always brings us back to the "terrific, most pitiable,
and maddening" image of Ahab as "a bird with clipped wing,
making affrighted broken circles in the air, vainly striving to
escape the piratical hawks" (298), as the lonely individual
cog in the great machine which has been broken beyond redemption. For Ahab's voice is above all the voice of the individual caught in the process of the great "creativeness mechanical," and Ahab's animal double can be seen in the image of the
old blind and crippled whale who has, unlike Ahab, "no voice"
to protest the "agony of fright" he must undergo to light the
lamps of the indifferent society that is made in the image of
the machine that grows the garden:

But pity there was none. For all his old age, and his one arm, and his blind
eyes, he must die the death and be murdered, in order to light the gay
bridals and other merry-makings of men, and also to illuminate the solemn
churches that preach unconditional inoffensiveness by all to all. [301]

Melville's comic vision is more complex, reflecting a greater
awareness of the ironies inherent in the natural order, than
those of Brown and Marcuse (p. 75), for the return to wholeness must go beyond animal innocence; Melville sees quite
clearly that the animals are no more free than mankind, that
their paths (like the broken, half-circular routes of the crippled
bird and whale) are if anything more "fixed" to "iron rails"
than Ahab's (147). Robert Ardrey, in his influential book *The
Territorial Imperative,* points out:

For the century or so since *Origin of Species* you and I and our fathers have been taught that the animal's only motivational pole is self. It is what we have meant by the struggle for existence and the survival of the fittest. . . . What has seemed inconceivable is that evolution could encourage any physical or behavioral trait running contrary to the interest of the individual: such behavior could have no survival value.

But as Freud had to abandon his "self-preservation" instinct, so geneticists have come to see, according to Ardrey, that "the basic evolutionary unit is not the individual but the population of which he is a part." This is called "population genetics," and Ardrey sees evolution enforcing a "biological morality" from which no animal is "free." The individual salmon is not free to ignore the homing impulse, even though it foredooms his individual death, and the Uganda Kob is not free to mate after losing to a dominant male in the "arena," because his "psychological castration" has been determined to be necessary to the natural selection process that insures the survival of the "population." Thus, the sexual behavior of animals is every bit as "organized" as that of humans, and the "flight from death" is just the human form of the biological morality that maintains the species at the expense of the individual.

So Ahab speaks for the individual, but not just against his inborn limitations or physical afflictions but also for his inborn possibilities. Ahab is obsessed by the irony that "in the midst of the personified impersonal, a personality stands here" (417). The impersonal machine of evolution has somehow produced a thinking, feeling personality, and Ahab would defend the right of that personality to resist the efforts of the Grim Reaper and Nirvana to make life, in Brown's phrase, "a more active form of dying."

There is, moreover, a biological rationale for Ahab's insistence on the need for defiance as the necessary balance to the attraction force of love. Brown suggests that Freud's theory of anxiety as a function of the fundamental "separation crises" inherent in all organic life is leading toward

a structural analysis of organic life as being constituted by a dialectic between unification or interdependence [Eros] and separation or independence [Thanatos]. The principle of unification or interdependence sustains the immortal life of the species and the mortal life of the individual; the principle of separation or independence gives the individual his individuality and ensures his death.

This is very close to Arthur Koestler's suggestion in *The Roots of Coincidence* that the two basic tendencies that pervade the organic and inorganic functioning "wholes" of the universe are the "integrative tendency" and the "self-assertive tendency." The keynote of his system is "equilibrium"; only through balance does the universe sustain itself:

The living organism and the body social [or atoms or galaxies] are not assemblies of elementary bits; they are multi-leveled, hierarchically organized systems of sub-wholes containing sub-wholes of a lower order, like Chinese boxes. These sub-wholes—or "holons," as I have proposed to call them—are Janus-faced entities which display both the independent properties of wholes and the dependent properties of parts. Each holon must preserve and assert its autonomy, otherwise the organism would lose its articulation and dissolve into an amorphous mass—but at the same time the holon must remain subordinate to the demands of the (existing or evolving) whole.

But Koestler sees one difference between the system as applied to animate as opposed to inanimate matter. While the universe may be running down like a machine, dissipating its energy according to the Second Law of Thermodynamics, "a living organism is all the time *building up* more complex chemicals from the chemicals it feeds on, more complex forms of energy from the energy it absorbs, and more complex patterns of information—perceptions, memories, ideas—from the input of its receptors. It is active instead of reactive."

All of this is implied in Ahab's championing of the superiority of the individual personality over the mechanisms that master it. And perhaps it suggests something of the nature of the "unsuffusing thing beyond" the more purely mechanical forces of the universe, and which only the evolved human imagination, through eyes "scorched" by the blank horrors of the machine, can "dimly see" (417). For Ahab's defiance is not self-assertion for its own sake but part of what Koestler calls "the quest for ultimate Unity, shared by the physicist, the mystic and the parapsychologist; a kind of unity which can only be attained by a detour through diversity, on a higher turn of the spiral . . . in the potentials of living matter to build up forms of greater complexity which display unity-in-variety on a higher level." But the individual psyche stops working toward this apotheosis when it gives itself up to an irremediable fear of death. Brown: "If death gives life individuality and if man is the organism which represses death, then man is the organism which represses his own individuality." Hence the need for a messiah who will render the grim image of death manageable again, who will also resist the Nirvana impulse that would "dissolve" the great, deep intellect into "an amorphous mass," who will show the way to making self-assertion serve not just self-preservation but higher forms of integration, who will restore to mankind, finally, something like Ishmael's "saving resolution," which marks as close as a whole man can come on the balance to the godlike indifference of broken Pip (347).

6

POE'S COSMOLOGY

Edgar Allan Poe, according to Arthur Hobson Quinn, numbered "A Descent into the Maelstrom" among his best stories. However, it has not received nearly as much critical attention as the other stories on Poe's list of favorites; it appears, in fact, to be a "problem" story. Those critics who have glossed the story seem to have ignored its deeper philosophical implications, even as they grope for an explanation of its profound effectiveness as an adventure-suspense story. I contend that the story derives its effectiveness not so much from the drama of the sailor's duel with the Maelstrom as from the vision he wins at its brink. It is, I believe, a vision of the nature of the cosmos and man's ordered place in it. Perhaps this story has proved such a puzzle to critics because they have not been ready to acknowledge the heavy reliance of Poe's fictional themes upon the philosophical and moral implications of his metaphysical speculations.

Poe outlined his inclusive theory of the design and nature of the cosmos in the long essay *Eureka* (1848) and his propositions on the nature of God in the essay/story "Mesmeric Revelation"; the action and theme of "A Descent into the Maelstrom" seem to proceed from such philosophical concerns

---

All parenthetical pagination in this chapter refers to either "A Descent into the Maelstrom," *Eureka, The Narrative of A. Gordon Pym,* "The Pit and the Pendulum," "The Fall of the House of Usher," or "The Imp of the Perverse" in *Edgar Allan Poe: Selected Prose, Poetry, and Eureka,* ed. W. H. Auden (New York: Holt, 1950).

as are presented in these works. Poe hints at this with his selection of a philosophical proposition from Joseph Glanvill for the story's epigraph, "The ways of God in Nature, as in Providence, are not as *our* ways" (131). The theme of the story, then, appears to be the how, why, and what-of-it of one man's discovery of God's ways in nature.

Poe's stories of suspense and horror are generally appreciated for their depths of psychological insight. And the psychological "single *effect*" of any of these stories is seen to proceed from Poe's strategic attempt to stimulate the reader's inner resources of terror. But it is often overlooked that the method in Poe's madness proceeds not simply from Poe's neurotic obsession with his own mental images of horror but also from his musings upon their mysterious role in the psychological fate of mankind. Certainly the sailor hero does not tell his tale of "the six hours of deadly terror" within the Maelstrom merely to watch his companion squirm; certainly the moral of his story is, as Poe's epigraph suggests, "commensurate to the vastness, profundity, and unsearchableness" of the universe in which mankind finds itself revolving.

Patrick F. Quinn, in his study *The French Face of Edgar Poe,* states that at least one critic, Camille Mauclair, has emphasized that Poe was essentially an *"idéologue,"* essentially a philosopher bent on unlocking "the secret of the world." And terror would seem to be the key: "Following the author's own lead in the matter, Mauclair insists that the element of terror in Poe's stories is not an end in itself, but only a theme, a pretext. Fear acts as a great mainspring of the psychological life, and only for this reason was Poe fascinated by it." Quinn balances this concept against his own observation that Poe's psychological obsession with "the dark torment of nightmare" works in dialectical opposition to his "lucid and inquiring" intellectual predisposition, "to bring up to the surface of . . . consciousness the kind of submerged emotional life that the intelligence prefers to ignore." The dialectic of terror and lucidity would appear to be at the motivating center of "A Descent into the Maelstrom."

The hero and his brother find themselves being drawn ineluctably into the surging water of the hurricane-whipped

Maelstrom. With their small fishing ship in the grip of this nightmarish phenomenon, the hero discovers himself to be in the grip of a force, parallel to that of the Maelstrom, equal in strength, which has arisen from within him. The force has arisen, presumably, from his "submerged emotional life," and he discovers that it has raw power enough to clench his eyelids together "as if in a spasm." He identifies the force as "terror," and he concludes that it has "unmanned" him, leaving him utterly incapable "of action or reflection" (142, 143).

Terror, then, has the power to strip a man of his powers of lucid inquiry and rational action. This motif recurs throughout Poe's stories; it is especially evident in *The Narrative of A. Gordon Pym*. Pym's story is of a perpetual inner struggle against the emotional chaos and paralysis of will that each new terrifying experience subjects him to. Following his narration of one such event that leaves him and Peters "weeping aloud like children," Pym comments upon their subsequent ability to overcome "privation and terror": "In subsequent perils, nearly as great, if not greater, I bore up with fortitude against all the evils of my situation, and Peters, it will be seen, evinced a stoical philosophy nearly as incredible as his present childlike supineness and imbecility—the mental condition made the difference" (260). Pym echoes Hamlet in his conviction that "the readiness is all," but the further implication behind his observation is that stoical self-control gives a man a certain power over his own fate. And this power, if we follow the mental process back to its source, appears to proceed from the individual's ability to achieve lucidity in the midst of the nightmare that is so central and pervasive a power in mankind's "submerged emotional life." The sailor hero achieves such a moment of lucidity in the depths of the Maelstrom and survives; his brother falls victim to the paralysis of terror and dies. The moral issue is thus drawn: one man driven by terror to an irrational attempt to save his life (he wrestles his brother away from the ringbolt), loses it; and the other, rational in his acceptance of the necessity to lose his life, saves it.

This dynamic, in varying forms, can be seen operating in many of Poe's stories, I believe; the moral tension is between chaos and order, hysteria and self-control, emotion and reason, and the movement of the hero's mind is between the freeze-framed, nightmarish paralysis of terror and the purposeful activity born of lucidity. For example, the narrator of "The Fall of the House of Usher" says of Roderick Usher, "To an anomalous species of terror I found him a bounden slave." Usher himself describes his condition in similar terms, "I feel that the period will sooner or later arrive when I must abandon life and reason together, in some struggle with the grim phantasm, Fear" (7). In the end he "*dared* not speak" (20), and in so doing he abandoned the lives of both himself and his sister to the paralytic nightmare. Contrast his fate to that of the nameless hero of "The Pit and the Pendulum," who describes, in terms similar to those of the sailor, how his eyes "closed themselves spasmodically at the descent" of the pendulum. He describes how at the height of his terror, "there suddenly came over my spirit all the keen, collected calmness of despair. For the first time during many hours—or perhaps days—I *thought*" (72). Some unnamed force, a match for the force of terror, arises from within his "submerged emotional life" and restores to him the lucidity necessary to divine the means of escape from the pendulum; it is the same force that allows the sailor the lucidity necessary to escape the Maelstrom.

In order to identify the source of this force and the source of the terror that opposes it, we must recognize that Poe conceived this psychological dialectic as analogous to, even as causally related to, the dialectical principles that he believed govern the nature and workings of the cosmos. The vision to be won from the mental struggle with terror on the brink of the abyss is a vision of a universe where the same laws that govern the paths of the planets govern the behavioral paths of human beings, just as surely and inextricably as the "ebony" walls of the Maelstrom guide the sailor's ship to its destiny. The sailor makes up his mind "to hope no more," and it is this decision that gives him the power to achieve the calmness of lucidity. The essence of such lucidity is a truer perspective of the nature of the universe and his own ordered place in it. He discovers "how magnificent a thing it was to die in such a manner, and how foolish it was in me to think of so paltry a consideration as my own individual life, in view of so wonderful a manifestation of God's power" (143). And so he becomes, in Melville's words, "uncompromised, indifferent as his God."

To understand the significance of the sailor's discovery and the dialectic that makes it the pathway to salvation, it is necessary to analyze Poe's cosmological vision. In *Eureka* Poe postulates that in the beginning God created "Matter in its utmost conceivable state of . . . Simplicity"; he continues:

Let us now endeavor to conceive what Matter must be, when, or if, in its absolute extreme of *Simplicity*. Here the Reason flies at once to Imparticularity—to a particle—to *one* particle—a particle of *one* kind—of *one* character—of *one* nature—of *one* size—of one form—a particle, therefore, "without form and void" . . . but positively a particle at all points. . . . [502]

This perfect unified matter exists so that it can be divided, and from the division arises the tension that gives form to the universe: God's volition was to separate the "One" into "Many"; the anticipated reaction of the Many is to seek to return into One. Thus, all matter becomes a manifestation of the dialectical principles of "Attraction," which Poe identified with the Newtonian theory of gravitation, and "Repulsion," identified as electricity. The pattern of the universe is diffusion but its origin is in unity, and thus, even as all matter has been "individualized" by the principle of repulsion (analogous to Koestler's "self-assertion"), all individualized matter has an innate affinity for all other individualized matter, and all atoms are moved by the principle of attraction (Koestler's "integration") and the possibility of reunification:

It is not to any *point* that the atoms are allied. It is not any *locality*, either in the concrete or in the abstract, to which I suppose them bound. Nothing like *location* was conceived as their origin. Their source lies in the principle, *Unity*. This is their lost parent. This they seek always—immediately—in all directions—wherever it is even partially to be found; thus appeasing, in some measure, the ineradicable tendency, while on the way to its absolute satisfaction in the end. [513]

It does not require further reflection to see that the Maelstrom provides the sailor with a vivid image of the primal tension that defines the physical nature of the universe. The ship does not simply plunge to the bottom of the abyss; it hangs suspended at an angle of "more than forty-five degrees," balanced between the forces of attraction and repulsion. The sailor discovers that he can walk upright as though the ship were sailing at "dead level." Gravity balances the inertia of centrifugal force; the ship travels like a planet around its sun; yet, the movement is inexorably around the center, closer and closer to the center, to the source; the principle of unity is at the helm. No wonder that the sailor finds the Maelstrom "so wonderful a manifestation of God's power." The Maelstrom seems almost to be a microcosm of the universe. Yet, Poe was not a transcendentalist; nature was not for him a symbol of spirit, nor was it a book to be read for its spiritual implications. How, then, should the reader interpret the phenomenon of the Maelstrom?

Poe conceived that various atom systems revolve around their "respective centres of aggregation" (*Eureka,* 584); unity is not a locality but a principle. The tension toward unity proceeds in all directions but always toward the same goal. Thus, any atom system is the mirror image of all other systems; galaxies mirror solar systems and solar systems, Maelstroms, because all these atomic systems are born in the same primal tension between the principles of attraction and repulsion, and Poe can thus conceive of the universe as an "endless extension of this system of cycles" around the motivating center of the universe. In this sense, then, "The Universe is a plot of God" (572), and the various systems of cycles are subplots that reflect back upon the grand design of the main plot. By catching the hero in the Maelstrom, God has presented the hero with a riveting dramatization of not only His plot for the universe but man's place in it. This is why the hero is so struck by the rainbow he sees in the depths of the Maelstrom; "the poetical instinct of humanity" (572) that Poe says is keyed into the essence of the universe is telling him that this is God's promise, as it was the sign of God's covenant with Noah, that the Maelstrom experience will somehow provide him with a "pathway between Time and Eternity" (145). The important question for mankind is, of course, How?

The answer is suggested in Poe's "Mesmeric Revelation." In the more rigidly argued *Eureka* Poe ducks the question of the nature and identity of God, but here he confronts the issue head-on:

> ... gradations of matter increase in rarity or fineness, until we arrive at a matter *unparticled*—without particles—indivisible—one; and here the law of impulsion [this seems equivalent to the attraction principle of *Eureka*] and permeation [repulsion, or electricity] is modified. The ultimate or unparticled matter, not only permeates all things but impels all things [toward unity, into itself]—and thus *is* all things within itself. This matter is God. What men attempt to embody in the word "thought" is this matter in motion.

Thus, God exists somehow as the manifestation of that un-particled matter that was at the beginning, and God is the source of unity toward which all individualized matter tends. God is the "perfection of matter," and this perfect, unparticled matter in motion is thought, and, "In general, this motion is the universal thought of the universal mind. This thought creates. All created things are but the thoughts of God."

The sailor hero and his brother are thoughts of God caught in the movement of the Maelstrom, another thought of God. Yet, the respective experiences of the two brothers seem to be in dialectical opposition. It would seem that the irrevocable thought "cycles" of the "universal mind" have provided a "pathway" to the hero that is not open to his brother. The key to the story, the essence of the moral dialectic, is, as I have suggested, the fact that the hero experiences a moment of lucidity in the midst of terror that his brother does not. Harry Levin has suggested in *The Power of Blackness* that this story differs from Poe's other sea stories, "Ms. Found in a Bottle" and *The Narrative of A. Gordon Pym,* in that here "the mind is enabled to exert control over matter." It is the *mind,* we now know, because in the moment of lucidity it becomes unparticled matter in motion; it becomes one with, is reunited with, the essence of God's thought. The unthinking mind, Poe suggests, remains the slave to the five "senses" that or-ganize physical reality for it. The hero's brother hears "the yell that went up to the Heavens from out of that mist," he feels the "wind and spray" that "blind, deafen, and strangle you," and the resulting terror elicited in him robs him of his ability for thought. The hero, however, becomes possessed of a Godlike "unnatural curiosity," his thoughts become a parallel phenomenon to the "rays of the full moon, from that circular rift amid the clouds," and the pattern of his thoughts, like the light of God's thoughts radiating from the moon, "streamed in a flood of golden glory along the black walls, and far away down into the inmost recesses of the abyss" (144–45).

At the moment of lucidity the hero's thoughts are vibrating in tune with the thoughts of the universal mind. This is possible because at the origin of the universe when God sent the spirit of diversity, the principle of repulsion, into the nature of all particled matter, He also found it necessary, according to Poe in "Mesmeric Revelation," to "incarnate portions of the divine mind" into that particled matter called man. Poe also postulates in "Mesmeric Revelation" that, as the human organism approaches death, it tends to move away from the organization of the sensual life and to become more in tune with the incarnate "universal mind" within itself (he calls this the "Heart Divine" in *Eureka,* 587), and, as this hitherto latent essence comes to life, it "vibrates" in "unison" with the "unparticled matter" which is the essence of the universe.

The movement of the sailor in the Maelstrom, then, can be interpreted as a movement from the periphery of God's thoughts ever and ever closer to their center, ever and ever closer to the more perfect motion of unity and wholeness; and, as he moves, his thoughts become more and more refined, approaching the perfection of the "unparticled" essence. It is thus no wonder that his old companions recognize him "no more than they would have known a traveller from the spirit-land" (148); for that is where his mind has been. The significance of his salvation parallels that of the resurrection of Jesus: it is a symbol of the reunification of man with God, only this time, as Feidelson has suggested, from the side of matter rather than spirit. Poe points out the parallel with Jesus' resurrection in the final sentence of the story. With quiet irony, the sailor tells his companion, "I can scarcely expect you to put more faith in it [his story] than did the merry fishermen of Lofoden." Jesus could just as readily have made the same comment in reference to the less merry but equally sceptical fishermen of Galilee, who did not recognize Him on *His* return (Luke 24:15–32).

It might be argued that it should be the hero's brother who achieves the final reunion with God since he is the one who travels the whole route of the Maelstrom to its center and to his own destruction. However, it must be remembered that his mind is frozen by the terror of the sensual life and can never, therefore, vibrate to the tune of the Maelstrom. The progress of the hero is as much mental as physical; he can thus travel closer to the unparticled essence of the Maelstrom, as is evidenced by the fact that he gains the ability to ascertain the mode of escape implicit in God's conception of the Maelstrom (he observes that cylindrical objects descend more slowly than any others, and so he lashes himself to a water cask, leaps overboard, and eventually bobs to the surface as the Maelstrom subsides). Since the Maelstrom is a thought of God, we can conceptualize it as being like a sentence; the hero's mind travels down its vortex the way a reader's eye follows the words of a subject–predicate–object configuration. The meaning of the sentence is not in the period that the reader's eye finally arrives at; it is in the thought generated by the words seen as a whole. Similarly, the essence of the Maelstrom is not to be found at its physical termination—the unifying center is not a locality, after all, but a principle—and it is toward the unifying principle that the hero's mind moves, while his body moves toward the physical center of the vortex.

But the ultimate question has still not been answered: What gives the hero the power to conquer terror and achieve the salvation of lucidity? In other words, what is the quality in his "submerged emotional life" that emerges in the Maelstrom and directs his incarnate mind to its "lost parent"? Poe does not seem to have fully conceptualized an answer, but his notion of "the imp of the perverse" signals the direction his thoughts were taking. In this story, more philosophical treatise than narrative, he argues that we should examine human behavior more in terms of what we witness man doing than in terms of what we assume God intends man to be doing. But this may cause more problems than it solves, since often we observe man acting "without comprehensible object," and we can go no further than to label this tendency as perversity. But, Poe argues, that the object is not visible does not mean that it does not exist. In fact, he continues, it seems that God has incorporated in our minds a *"force* which impels us," "a primitive impulse—elementary." He likens it to the force which impels a man when, standing upon the brink of an abyss shrinking from the imagined horror of the fall, the man still vividly desires the fall, and, says Poe, "There is no passion in nature so demonically impatient, as that of him who shuddering upon the edge of a precipice, thus meditates a plunge" ("The Imp of the Perverse," 91–92). The sailor cannot experience lucidity until the imp of the perverse instills in him a *"wish"* ("Maelstrom," 143) to "sacrifice" his life for a moment's exploration of the bottom of the abyss. Similarly, Pym finds himself at one point hanging over a cliff on a rope. In the grip of terror, vividly imagining "the rushing and headlong descent" should his hands slip from the rope, he finds himself possessed of a strangely perverse, seemingly instinctual desire: "And now I was consumed with the irrepressible desire of looking below. I could not, I would not, confine my glances to the cliff; and, with a wild, indefinable emotion, half of horror, half of relieved oppression, I threw my vision far down into the abyss." And at that moment, he continues, "my whole soul was pervaded with a *longing to fall;* a desire, a yearning, a passion utterly uncontrollable." He gives himself up to this desire, swoons, and is caught at the last moment by Peters. Upon waking he makes the startling discovery that "my trepidation had entirely vanished; I felt a new being" (325). The imp of the perverse is, then, a preliminary psychological manifestation of the metaphysical principle of attraction, which has been lying dormant but which activates somehow as the individual approaches, in a time of danger and death, what Mailer calls "the existential edge," and which has the power to return the individual to the "new" condition, invested with all the divine powers of a thinking mind in unparticled motion.

Marie Bonaparte, in *The Life and Work of Edgar Allan Poe: A Psychoanalytic Interpretation,* was the first to identify Poe's "imp of the perverse" with Freud's concept of Thanatos, the death instinct. She identifies the Maelstrom as a womb image and the hero's desire to explore its depths as "a version of the return-to-the-womb phantasy"; she apparently resisted the temptation to comment on the phallic resonances of the cylindrical water cask. By this interpretation, then, the death instinct is that force that activates lucidity. And Eros, the life instinct, by implication, would be the force that resists the pull of the abyss; terror would seem to be the tool that the life instinct employs to keep the individual deaf to the siren song of the death instinct.

Such a neat and clean Freudian superstructure is very beguiling, and it has beguiled me. However, as was pointed out in chapter 5, Freud's life-versus-death dialectic is more prone to paradox than to simplicity. Paradoxically, it is the sailor's brother's resistance to death that, in fact, insures his death. Poe like Melville is preoccupied not with death but the fear of death, the Grim Reaper image that paralyzes both body and mind. The distinctly human dialectic that emerges in the Maelstrom, the central difference between the sailor and his brother, is not attraction versus repulsion, but the universal neurosis of mankind: Nirvana versus the Grim Reaper. The pull of Nirvana, the imp of the perverse, saves the hero from the Grim Reaper, the narcissistic paralysis of terror, but as the hero's mind begins to reflect on the pattern of the universe, he becomes strong enough mentally to resist, as well, the fatal urge of Nirvana to "erotize death." This is what Roderick Usher is not strong enough to do. It would take an Ernest Jones to do justice to the phallic imagery of this story, to the "decayed trees" and the gray "turrets" and Ethelred's mace, to the "deep and dank tarn" that envelops the fissured house, and to such phrases as the "rending of her coffin" and the "blood upon her white robes." The imagery suggests the longing of unconsummated incestuous love and the "cataleptic character" (14) that is born in the palpable presence of the Grim Reaper, in "the home" of one's vengeful "forefathers" (12).

Too fearful of "a family evil" to embrace each other in life, brother and sister erotize death instead, and so allow themselves to be drawn slowly and in agony to an embrace in death.

The Grim Reaper versus Nirvana seems the unregenerate human form of the universal dialectic, repulsion versus attraction. And the sailor's salvation signifies the passing of an individual human mind from the one state to the other; the evidence is in the balance that he achieves. The "mere instinct," self-preservation (the unregenerate form of repulsion), that causes him and then his brother to grasp blindly at the ring-bolt, gives way to an equally blind "wish" for the bottom of the abyss (the unregenerate form of attraction), but this in turn is transformed into an "unnatural curiosity" (the regenerate form of attraction) that "appeared to grow upon me as I drew nearer and nearer to my dreadful doom" (146), and which allows him to resist physically what he seeks mentally. The imp of the perverse, the death wish, has led the sailor to a mental vision of the grand design, and it is toward this vision, not annihilation, that he is attracted. And with the transcending vision comes the godlike detachment of the mind in motion: "I even sought *amusement* in speculating upon the relative velocities of [objects descending in the Maelstrom]." So his leap overboard is not blind self-preservation but a reasoned act (arising "partly from memory, and partly from present observation") of self-assertion or repulsion.

Paradoxically, again, it is the sailor's surrender to death that leads to the saving of his life. But the death wish or imp of the perverse must not be confused with the principle of attraction which has been identified with Koestler's "integrative tendency" (p. 87), which, in turn, has been identified with Freud's Eros (p. 81). In fact, Poe's metaphysics suggests a solution to the riddle Freud could never solve: the complex interdependence of the instinctual opposites, life and death. In *Eros and Civilization* Marcuse explains how the puzzle emerges from Freud's speculations in *Beyond the Pleasure Principle*:

Freud is driven to emphasize time and again the common nature of the instincts [life and death] prior to their differentiation. The outstanding and frightening event is the discovery of the fundamental *regressive* or "conservative" tendency in all instinctual life. Freud cannot escape the suspicion that he has come upon a hitherto unnoticed "universal attribute of the instincts and perhaps of organic life in general," namely, "a compulsion inherent in organic life to restore an earlier state of things which the living entity has been obliged to abandon under the pressure of external disturbing forces"—a kind of "organic elasticity" or "inertia inherent in organic life." This would be the ultimate content or substance of those "primary processes" which Freud from the beginning recognized as operating in the unconscious. They were first designated as the striving for "the free outflow of the quantities of excitation".... But more and more the inner logic of the conception asserts itself. Constant freedom from excitation has been finally abandoned at the birth of life; the instinctual tendency toward equilibrium thus is ultimately regression behind life itself. The primary processes of the mental apparatus, in their striving for integral gratification, seem to be fatally bound to the "most universal endeavor of all living substance—namely to return to the quiescence of the inorganic world." The instincts are drawn into the orbit of death.

Freud sees the trap he is falling into and tries to avoid it with a very tentative return to myth and metaphysics. In *Beyond the Pleasure Principle* he takes Plato's myth of the hermaphrodite (explained by Aristophanes in *The Symposium* as the being divided in two by Zeus, the *whole* being, that is, which males and females seek to reinstate in their sexual coupling) and attempts to put it on a naturalistic basis:

Are we to follow the clue of the poet-philosopher and make the daring assumption that living substance was at the time of its animation rent into small particles, which since that time strive for reunion by means of the sexual instincts? That these instincts—in which the chemical affinity of inanimate matter is continued—passing through the realm of the protozoa gradually overcome all hindrances set to their striving by an environment charged with stimuli dangerous to life, and are impelled by it to form a protecting covering layer? And that these dispersed fragments of living substance thus achieve a multi-cellular organization, and finally transfer to the germ-cells in a highly concentrated form the instinct for reunion?

Freud seems to be suggesting that the differentiated organism protects itself from dissolution in order to save itself for ultimate dissolution. His problem is with the assumptions of the old science for which the "regression behind life itself" can be nothing other than a return to the state of what Freud calls "*in*animate matter." Freud cannot get over thinking of the instincts as blind, unreasoning forces acting on the psyche as Newton's principle of "inertia" (as explained by Marcuse, above) acts on celestial bodies. But the new science suggests that the organic drive toward unification (as in Poe's "attraction" or Koestler's "integrative tendency") displays a transcending *intelligence* at even the most primitive organic level. For example, in *The Roots of Coincidence* Koestler describes John Bleibtreu's study of the "behavior" of the slime mold, which is "an amoeba which lives on bacteria found among the decaying leaves in forests" and "multiplies by simple cell division every few hours." When threatened by starvation, the "amoeba stop behaving as individuals and aggregate into groups," becoming in Koestler's words "a literal metaphor for the organization of cells in a multi-celled individual." Most incredibly, the aggregation achieves a functioning form which then migrates across the floor of the forest, in the direction of light and heat, until a sustaining environment is found. Koestler's implication, of course, is: if such miraculous powers of integration, if such intelligence, can be found at this level, how much greater they must be at the human level of development.

Poe's metaphysics, so close to the new science in assumptions, puts the formulation this way: how much closer man, the thinking animal, must be to a reunification with the unparticled wholeness out of which we came. Poe's cosmogony, so close in conception to the "big bang" (George Gamow's phrase) theory of modern astrophysicists, corrects Freud's by envisioning the primal state of wholeness as a state of a more "perfect" animation, and so it is not death that the thinking mind seeks beyond life but this unparticled state of wholeness. Poe, unlike Freud, puts his faith in the central intelligence that guides the particled human intelligence to its "lost parent."

One man dies; the other lives, and in living becomes the literal incarnation of Ishmael's Catskill eagle, lured by "the blackest gorges" but still balanced enough to "soar out of them again and become invisible in the sunny spaces." Buoyed to the surface by a wooden vessel resembling Ishmael's life-sustaining coffin, the resurrected sailor represents the resolution of the moral issue raised by the story, which develops out of Poe's observation that man has the capability to purify his thought, to vibrate in tune with God's thought, while still revolving on the brink of the abyss, on this side of ultimate reunification. Man achieves the capability to think rationally, to act morally, even to determine his own destiny, Poe seems to be implying, to the extent that he can free his mind from the chains of terror, to the extent that he can approximate in his actions the motions of God's thought, to the extent that he can mirror in his mind the cosmic balance between attraction and repulsion, to the extent that he is "ready," in Mailer's words, "to share the dread of the Lord."

7

ELLISON'S

CHATTERING-MONKEY BLUES

The visionary writer in America, as I have said, belongs to an intellectual tradition, but one that is curiously drawn to the vagaries of the emotional life. Hence Melville, the champion of the "great, deep intellect," could write to Hawthorne on 16 April 1851, "I stand for the heart. To the dogs with the head!" And Poe could dedicate *Eureka,* his hymn to the mind in motion, to those "who feel rather than to those who think." But, as Patrick Quinn has observed of Poe, this is more a dialectic than a contradiction (p. 84).

The same dialectic is the motivating center of Ralph Ellison's *Invisible Man.* Ellison, after Poe, is the American writer most self-consciously committed to the idea of the mind thinking, of the mind, that is, as the ultimate source of transcendence or salvation. But he is also the inheritor of a wellspring of emotional pain, the collective black experience in America, that has received its traditional artistic expression in the blues beat and lyric. Several critics, including Edward Margolies, Gene Bluestein, Raymond M. Olderman, Robert Bone, Tony Tanner, and Ellison himself have emphasized the influence of blues forms and themes on the structure of the novel, but some of these critics, perhaps wishing for Ellison to be more black

---

Parenthetical pagination in this chapter refers to either *Invisible Man* (New York: NAL, 1952) or to *Shadow and Act* (New York: NAL, 1966).

than American, have not given proper emphasis to its intellectual framework.

In fact, the novel amounts to a critique of both the intellectual and the emotional dimensions of the American experience. The Brotherhood (an obvious pseudonym for the Communist Party), which prides itself on its "reasonable point of view" and "scientific approach to society" (304), represents the *head* of the social structure, as do also such characters as Bledsoe, Norton, Emerson, and all who think without feeling; and characters like Trueblood, Emerson Jr., Lucius Brockway, Tarp, Tod Clifton, and Ras, all those who feel without thinking, represent the *heart*. Given the two dimensions, the invisible man's problem, as for the heroes of the other writers studied here, is "How to Be!" And, as with the others, salvation is the attainment of a balance, of a unification of mind and body, thought and feeling, idea and action, that forms a pattern of existence with the potential to transcend the "biological morality" (Ardrey's term) imposed from within and the social morality imposed from without.

Melville saw all men "enveloped in whale lines"; it is Ellison's vision that all men, whether powerful or weak, are puppets controlled by invisible strings ("the force that pulls your strings," 137), like Clifton's dancing Sambo doll (386). Ellison's vision is of a complex chattering-monkey society composed of blind, mindless puppets wearing the masks assigned to them, playing the roles demanded of them, striking out blindly at the targets provided for them. A metaphor for this society is the battle royal (see 323, "suddenly alive in the dark with the horror of the battle royal"), in which the young black boys are set plunging and swinging wildly about a boxing ring. Blindfolded, they fight "hysterically," in a "confused" state of "terror" and "hate," while not one blow reaches the southern whites who are the makers of their pain and confusion (24–28). Tatlock comes to believe in the game, as the vet doctor will later warn the invisible man not to do (137), comes to believe that by striking at his comrade, the youthful invisible man, he is striking at a representative of the whites (by virtue of the invisible man's college scholarship). Ironically, one of the white men has to remind the invisible man that he is nothing but a "Sambo" (29).

Tatlock and the invisible man use each other as scapegoats, and the invisible man will go on to strike out at a long string of scapegoats, each representing a different social or political affiliation (Bledsoe, Brockway, Ras, Brother Jack), will himself serve as a scapegoat for all these groups, before he is finally driven from society by an ironic amalgamation of black revolutionaries and white reactionaries. The invisible man is accused of treachery by the spokesmen of every group represented in the novel (see especially the denunciations of Bledsoe, Ras, and Brother Jack; 124, 326, 403), is haunted by his grandfather's confession to having been a "traitor" to his people (20), is overcome by the irony that even his grandfather's formula for avoiding treachery ("overcome 'em with yeses") leads him to betray his race ("A tool just at the very moment I had thought myself free. By pretending to agree I had indeed agreed . . . , " 478). The ultimate question in Ellison is: To what "society of gods" can the "dispossessed" (300) reverse-*pharmakos* give ultimate allegiance?

Ellison differs from the other writers discussed here in that he envisions no unifying force at the center of the cosmos; where the others see a pattern of meaning on which to build what Ellison calls a "plan of living," Ellison sees only "chaos." The human problem then becomes how "to give pattern to the chaos which lives within the pattern" of the "certainties" (502) upon which blind men have built their societies. In *Symbolism and American Literature* Charles Feidelson calls Poe's philosophy "materialistic idealism." Allowing for the same possibility of a contradiction in terms, Ellison's philosophy might be called existential transcendentalism. As he told John O' Brien in *Interviews with Black Writers,* "Human life is a move toward the rational. Whatever man must do in order to bring order to the society is what he considers rational. For a moralist, the problem is to point out that such order is not imposed by nature and it is not imposed by God. It's a human thing." In other words, just as man creates his own damnation, he must create his own salvation, just as man has spent his existence imposing pseudorational strings on himself, he must train himself to be true to the truly rational. He goes on to tell O'Brien:

> in a political system you are going to end up with some form of inequality. But in just the nature of things there are going to be some who are more equal than others and some who are less equal. The human challenge is to moderate this and you can only do this by consciously keeping the ideal alive, by not treating it as a folly, but by treating it as Thoreau and Emerson were treating it, as a conscious discipline which imposed upon you a conscientiousness which made you aware, every hour and every day. To impose a human vision upon the world ... but it's so easy to drift.

Therefore, the invisible man discovers that salvation is ultimately a function of "the *mind*" (502), and his allegiance passes over to an ethereal realm of intellectual principles. In reflecting on his grandfather's cryptic deathbed advice, he decides that

> he *must* have meant the principle, that we were to affirm the principle on which the country was built and not the men, or at least not the men who did the violence. Did he mean to say "yes" because he knew that the principle was greater than the men, greater than the numbers and the vicious power and all the methods used to corrupt its name? Did he mean to affirm the principle, which they themselves had dreamed into being out of the chaos and darkness of the feudal past, and which they had violated to the point of absurdity even in their own corrupt minds? Or did he mean that we had to take the responsibility for all of it, for the men as well as the principle, because we were the heirs who must use the principle because no other fitted our needs? Not for the power or for vindication, but because we, with the given circumstances of our origin, could only thus find transcendence? [497]

The principle, Ellison told O'Brien, is "democracy," and the passage of the hero out of the society where democracy is merely the mask that oppression wears becomes a two-stage, up-from-one's-own-bootstraps process in which his emotions purify his "corrupt" mind and his purified mind gives him the perspective necessary to transcend his emotions. The invisible man discovers, almost too late, that the Brotherhood's ideal of reaching people "through their intelligence" is the mask for a sinister, paternalistic policy of taking advantage of people "in their own best interest" (436), the mirror image, in fact, of the school superintendent's and Bledsoe's policy of leading the people "in the proper paths" (33). The true principle, of which these are a corruption, can be discovered only at the conclusion of an arduous rite of passage through the under-world (expressed metaphorically by ubiquitous images of tunnels, subways, and basement rooms; cf. 15, 57, 181, 379–83), through the "lower frequencies" (503) of the human psyche where the blues originates, the unconscious world of primitive human emotions and instincts where the thinking man discovers that beneath the social and racial allegiances he is "linked to all the others in the loud, clamoring semi-visible world" (497).

The American black man, Ellison seems to be suggesting, is in a special position to achieve the balance of thought and feeling, of responsibility and freedom necessary for "transcendence" over society's death grip on the individual unconscious. On the one hand, owing to the "given circumstances" of his "origin," the blues experience, he has had "not much, but some" of the "human greed and smallness" and "fear and superstition" (497), which has corrupted the white mind, burned out of him. On the other hand, to remain isolated from the intellectual patterns that structure history (253), isolated in an albeit free world of pure feeling, is to remain in "that world seen only as a fertile field for exploitation by Jack and his kind, and with condescension by Norton and his" (497). The blues experience has purified the emotions of the black man, Ellison seems to be saying, but unless his mind can learn to see the meaning underlying the blues form, and to take the responsibility for his own salvation, he will never be able to transcend the imprisoning social structure.

The theme of the blues is emotional pain, not as triumphed over, but as lived with, endured. In "Richard Wright's Blues" Ellison defines the blues as

an impulse to keep the painful details and episodes of a brutal experience alive in one's aching consciousness, to finger its jagged grain, and to transcend it, not by the consolation of philosophy but by squeezing from it a near-tragic, near-comic lyricism. As a form it is an autobiographical chronicle of personal catastrophe expressed lyrically. [90]

In the same essay he suggests that the blues expression of the southern Negro is the only response possible in his violence-prone world, "the consolation of philosophy" having been denied to him:

In the North energies are released and given *intellectual* channelization—energies which in most Negroes in the South have been forced to take either a *physical* form or, as with potentially intellectual types like [Richard] Wright, to be expressed as nervous tension, anxiety and hysteria.... The human organism responds to environmental stimuli by converting them into either physical and/or intellectual energy. And what is called hysteria is suppressed intellectual energy expressed physically. [99]

And what is called the blues would seem to be the resulting hysteria expressed lyrically.

Ellison associates the blues and the black experience with the hysteria of "confusion," a motif which recurs again and again in the novel (14, 63, 168, 170, 208, 240, 338, 344, 383); it is the confusion that arises, presumably, from suppressing intellectual energy. Take Trueblood, for example:

"I thinks and thinks, until I thinks my brain go'n bust, bout how I'm guilty and how I ain't guilty.... Finally, one night, way early in the mornin', I looks up and sees the stars, and I starts singin'. I don't mean to, I didn't think 'bout it, just start singin'.... All I know is I *ends up* singin' the blues." [63]

Similarly, without thinking about it, the invisible man finds himself echoing the blues refrain of Louis Armstrong, "What did I do/To be so black/And blue?" (15, 168), after he discovers, but cannot understand, the "joke" played on him by Bledsoe; later he hears himself humming a forgotten blues refrain, "O well they picked poor Robin clean," and he says, "My mind seized upon the tune" (170), rather than upon the ideas of the tune, presumably.

Confusion is in turn linked to what Raymond M. Olderman in "Ralph Ellison's Blues and *Invisible Man*" calls the "scapegoat" motif of the blues. Super-Cargo (superego), for example, represents internalized white authority ("the white folks' man") to the mental patients in the Golden Day ("Sometimes I get so afraid of him I feel he's inside my head"), and when given the opportunity to express their suppressed intellectual energy physically, they instinctively attack him and not Mr. Norton. But the vet doctor warns Norton that with Super-Cargo mastered,

> They might suddenly realize that you are what you are, and then your life wouldn't be worth a piece of bankrupt stock. You would be cancelled, perforated, voided, become the recognized magnet attracting loose screws. . . . To some you are the great white father, to others the lyncher of souls, but for all, you are *confusion* come even into the Golden Day. [85-86, my italics]

Both Super-Cargo and Norton represent some truth beyond the limited roles they play in the social structure, but since the blues mentality of the inmates is not prone to intellectual analysis, a symbolically appropriate scapegoat satisfies the emotional demands of the occasion ("Try it, schoolboy, it feels so good. It gives you relief," 78).

In the absence of an intellectual framework, the scapegoat motif gives form to their protest, just as the scapegoat gives form to the melodrama (pp. 47–48). A similar theme appears in Eudora Welty's brilliant short story "Powerhouse" (1941). The blues singer Powerhouse improvises a talking blues about the imagined suicide of his wife. Responsible in some vague, indistinct way is a "no-good pussy-footed crooning creeper" named Uranus Knockwood, who seems the personification of the nebulous force that "take our wives when we gone." But Powerhouse confesses to a credulous waitress when she asks, "No, Babe, it ain't the truth. . . . Truth is something worse—I ain't said what, yet. It's something hasn't come to me, but I ain't saying it won't." Similarly, the vet doctor explains that the paranoiac's universal, unnamed "They" is the legitimate expression of the "truth" as "most men feel" it (137–38) but which is "never there" when the mind tries to pin it down.

In *Natives Sons* Edward Margolies has described Ellison's hero/narrator as a blues "singer," who sings "a record of past wrongs, pains, and defeats," each episode serving "almost as an extended blues verse." While the novel is certainly an episodic account of painful defeats at the hands of a number of different scapegoat figures, Margolies, who seems to see blues as the sole structuring purpose of the novel, fails to recognize that the invisible man comes to reject the illogic of the blues form when he realizes that he has become a scapegoat for Ras. He rejects the role, even though he feels in part "responsible" (478) for the misguided riot, because he understands just how inappropriate and irrational his selection is ("He held me responsible for all the nights and days and all the suffering and for all that which I was incapable of controlling"):

I looked at Ras on his horse and at their handful of guns and recognized the absurdity of the whole night and of the simple yet confoundingly complex arrangement of hope and desire, fear and hate, that had brought me here still running, and knowing that I had no longer to run for or from the Jacks and the Emersons and the Bledsoes and Nortons, but only from their *confusion,* impatience, and refusal to recognize the beautiful absurdity of their American identity and mine. [483, my italics]

His mind has developed to the point where, like Powerhouse and unlike the waitress, he can separate the personifications from the principles they represent. But the frightening discovery is that this "confoundingly complex arrangement" of marionette strings has corrupted even the black man's treasured emotional heritage.

Just as Ellison links confusion to the blues, he in turn links the blues to the nature of southern Negro preaching. At the lowest level of his blues reverie in the prologue, the invisible man finds a black preacher perpetuating confusion by patterning the words of his sermon on the emotional response of his congregation rather than on any pattern demanded by the sense of their meaning: *"'Black will git you . . .'/'Yes it will'/ '. . . an' black won't . . .'/'Naw, it won't!'/'It do . . .'/'It do, Lawd'/'. . . an' it don't' "* (12–13). In the chapel, reflecting on the kind of preaching and debating that has gone on there, he describes it as "more sound than sense, a play upon the resonances of buildings, an assault upon the temples of the ear . . . *old connoisseur of voice sounds, of voices without messages . . . a river of word-sounds filled with drowned passions . . . the sound of words that were no words . . .*" (102–3). But, ironically, it is precisely the invisible man's gift for the sound of words that the Brotherhood will harness to its corrupt purpose. As the rich Sister tells him: "You have tom-toms beating in your voice." He replies with weak humor that he "thought that was the beat of profound ideas" (357). But, of course, he never thinks about what he is going to say before he says it; he only puzzles over its effect on the emotions of his audience after he has said it. In fact, his speeches are all potential failures until he discards rational development for the ebb and flow of a blues refrain or motif: "What are we to do?" (240), "We are the uncommon people" (297). Brother Jack rebukes the invisible man at one point by telling him, "You were not hired to think" (405), which seems an inappropriate thing to say to a lecturer, but of course he was hired to sing the blues. Like the "record shop loudspeaker" which he hears "blaring a languid blues" after Clifton's death, his only contribution to the "history of the times" is a "mood," expressed in words that are at once "turgid" and "inadequate" (383).

Society, to return to Norman O. Brown for a moment, is constructed "from defect, from death and the flight from death, from fear of separation and fear of individuality" (p. 69). Ellison shares Brown's Freudian understanding of mankind's sense of its own insufficiency, a sense that motivates the "simple yet confoundingly complex arrangement of hope and desire, fear and hate." The marionette strings project outward from the collective unconscious to confuse not only the black man's feelings but the society's truest principles.

The "escape" of the hero from the regressive patriarchy of the South (i.e., "the cold Father symbol of the Founder," 37) to the more egalitarian North is an ontogenetic recapitulation of the phylogenesis of Western society; it mirrors the transformation of the "primal horde," in Freud's formulation, into the "brother horde." The "Brotherhood" (dropping the "r" in horde) represents the new cooperative society (the first act of cooperation being the murder of the father). The father's domination, according to Freud in *Moses and Monotheism,* was brutal:

> The strong male was the master and father of the whole horde, unlimited in his power, which he used brutally. All females were his property, the wives and daughters in his own horde. . . . The fate of the sons was a hard one; if they excited the father's jealousy they were killed or castrated or driven out.

The invisible man threatens the authority of Bledsoe and is driven out (a clue to Ellison's plot source is the copy of *Totem and Taboo* lying open on Emerson Jr.'s desk, 159). But the implicit irony of the brother horde is that one cannot transcend the father, and to murder the father is merely to institutionalize murder, and thereby perpetuate the need to murder the father. Freud continues:

> It is a reasonable surmise that after the killing of the father a time followed when the brothers quarreled among themselves for the succession, which each of them wanted to obtain for himself alone. They came to see that these fights were as dangerous as they were futile. . . . Thus there came into being the first form of a social organization accompanied by a renunciation of instinctual gratification; recognition of mutual obligations; institutions declared sacred, which could not be broken—in short, the beginnings of morality and law. Each renounced the ideal of gaining for himself the position of father, of possessing his mother or sister. With this the taboo of incest and the law of exogamy came into being. . . . The memory of the father lives on during this time of the "brother horde." A strong animal, which perhaps at first was also dreaded, was found as a substitute. . . . The relationship to the totem animal retained the original ambivalency of feeling toward the father . . . he was to be revered and protected. On the other hand, a festival was instituted on which day the same fate was meted out to him as the primeval father had encountered. He was killed and eaten by all the brothers together. . . .

The totem feast, similar in intent to the ancient practice of scapegoating (Leviticus 16:20–22), is given a strictly American dimension by Ellison. In his blues reverie the invisible man encounters a slave woman who has loved her master for giving her "several sons" and hated him for not setting them free; she has murdered the planter before "them boys" can tear their father "to pieces with they homemake knives." The dreaming invisible man is "confused" as the brothers celebrate their new "freedom." "A mistake was made somewhere," he says (14). This retelling of the primal horde myth in blues form seems a reference to the "mistake" made by Ras when he becomes the Destroyer. Ras thinks he is freeing his black "Brothers" (321) from the white enslavers, but in reality he can do nothing other than set up a new brother horde, merely exchanging one set of scapegoat and totem figures for another. Meanwhile the "memory of the father" lives on. As Frye has demonstrated in "Theory of Modes," the scapegoat figure represents "less an attack on a virtuous society by a malignant individual than a symptom of that society's viciousness." Ultimately, Ellison has written in "Richard Wright's Blues," the blues offers "no scapegoat but the self," (104) the self that discovers "on the lower frequencies" that it is "linked to all the others" by a shared heritage of fear and viciousness. That is the "beautiful absurdity" of the "American identity," and that, the invisible man discovers, is the meaning of the blues.

But the brother horde can work only if the shared heritage is denied. So, when a universal desire surfaces somewhere, as in the case of Trueblood's incest, it must be treated as a gross perversion and the offending individual excised brutally from the community, made a symbolic scapegoat. The blues is a danger to the social fabric because of its emphasis on the commonality of human emotions (when Powerhouse finishes his blues, for example, "Everybody in the room moans with reassurance," having heard "put into words," as the vet doctor tells Crenshaw, "things which most men feel," 138). For this reason Trueblood can bear the "guilt" heaped upon him. By making him feel the universality of his emotions (note his association of his act with the similarly sociopathic act of shooting it out with the police in Birmingham, 58), the blues has led him to face and accept the fear that society is constructed to deny: the fear of individuality ("I makes up my mind that I ain't nobody but myself," 63). The invisible man comes to a similar conclusion after he rejects the scapegoat role that Brother Jack would have him play; he reflects on his blues experience, his "images of past humiliations," and he decides: "They were me; they defined me. I was my experiences and my experiences were me" (439).

But there is a danger in emotional freedom. There really is a "chaos" out there on the borders of society; an individual needs "a socially responsible role to play" (503), or he will revert in his "cynicism" (436) to the barbaric condition of anarchy and chaos, where the unconscious rules unrestrained by anything except necessity. This is what the invisible man calls "Rinehartism"; "Rine the runner and Rine the gambler and Rine the briber" seems at first to be the essence of individual "possibility" (430); his "possibility" seems to be the antidote to the "social responsibility" (32) preached by society, which turns out to mean nothing more than the "SACRIFICE" (410) of the individual. But Ellison understands that the social morality (the brother horde) is ultimately determined by the biological morality (the primal horde) that enslaves us all and that there cannot be, therefore, any ultimate freedom from, only moderation of, evil and pain.

When the individual submits to society's ideal of responsibility, the *"uncreated features of his face,"* the surface idiosyncrasies that make him different from all other men, remain uncreated (307). In Aristotelian terms, he is all substance and no form. Since this "formless" (10) man is invisible to both others and himself, he must wear a mask assigned to him, as the invisible man does throughout the novel, merely exchanging one mask for another as his affiliations shift. However, when the individual becomes too free from responsibility, when his possibilities are without limit, he becomes nothing but face, all form and no substance, having denied the common substance that makes him one with all other men. The cynical Dr. Bledsoe, who cares for nothing but his own personal "power" (129), has one face for the white folks and one for the black folks (93), is the slave to the demands required of those faces, but has no face of his own. And Rinehart has no discernible substance whatsoever; he is a disembodied composite portrait, drawn from the various roles he plays.

The invisible man transcends the dangers of the dialectical opposites, collective responsibility and individual possibility, by achieving a synthesis of them. Thus, he drives Brother Jack into a frenzy when he espouses a new, balanced ideal called "personal responsibility" (400, 410). He becomes a whole man, both substance and form, body and mind, emotion and reason when he learns how to balance between what Robert M. Pirsig in *Zen and the Art of Motorcycle Maintenance* calls his "duty toward others" and his "duty toward himself." For example, after his final confrontation with Jack, he decides in his cynicism to become all face, to start yessing them to death. To get his feet wet, he takes up with a disgusting white woman named Sybil, who is consumed by a secret desire to be raped by a black "buck." Like all prejudices, hers denies his individuality, denies the idiosyncrasies of his own face for the gross features of the mask she would have him wear. He seems completely justified when he attempts to humiliate her by scrawling a message in lipstick on her bare stomach after she passes out. But then he says to himself, "Such games were for Rinehart, not me," and he washes it off. He has looked beneath the surface of her perverse, idiosyncratic sexual desires and has recognized a common humanity in the strange masks each of their most basic desires has assumed. As she has needed to be raped by a black man, he has needed to humiliate a white woman. From that point on he humors her perversity, even protects her from it when she strives blindly to become part of the rape and pillage in Harlem that night. He, and he alone, acting as an individual, has accepted responsibility for her:

I looked at her out of a deep emptiness and refilled her glass and mine. What had I done to her, allowed her to do? Had all of it filtered down to me? My action . . . my—the painful word formed as disconnectedly as her wobbly smile—my *responsibility?* [454-55]

So he will not accept the scapegoat role society has chosen for him to play, but neither will he overstay his "hibernation" in an underground world of pure possibility. The promise of the invisible man is that he will emerge with enough balance to articulate the feelings that we all have locked in our minds (the old slave woman's definition of "freedom" is *"nothing but knowing how to say what I got up in my head,"* 14; see also 335). And, if he can speak for poor warped Sybil, he can even speak "for you" (503).

8

MAILER'S COSMOLOGY

Norman Mailer began his career writing safely within the American naturalistic tradition. *The Naked and the Dead* (1948), according to M. H. Abrams in *A Glossary of Literary Terms,* is characteristic of novels written within the tradition that takes as its premise the "post-Darwinian" notion that

man belongs entirely in the order of nature and does not have a soul or any other connection with a religious or spiritual world beyond nature; that man is therefore merely a higher-order animal whose character and fortunes are determined by two kinds of natural forces, heredity and environment. He inherits his personal traits and his compulsive instincts, especially hunger and sex, and he is subject to the social and economic forces in the family, the class and the milieu into which he is born.

Such an understanding of human motivation has seemed a broad enough vision of the human condition for many of our most important twentieth-century writers. And few, especially since the rise of existentialism, seem to have needed to fall back on older conceptions of the spiritual or the supernatural in presenting their narratives.

In his two novels of the 1960s, however, Norman Mailer

Parenthetical pagination in this chapter refers to either *An American Dream* (New York: Dell, 1966), *Why Are We in Vietnam?* (New York: Putnam, 1968), or "The White Negro," *Advertisements for Myself* (New York: Berkley, 1966).

seems to have transformed modern naturalistic and existential insights into a new vision of the supernatural forces that give pattern to man's "heredity and environment." The first of these novels, *An American Dream*, attempts an answer to a question the detective Leznicki asks, "Why'd you kill her, Rojack?" (72). Had Rojack been ready to submit to a merely human authority, the most valid reply he could make would be with another question, *Why Are We in Vietnam?* the title of the second novel. Both questions have the same answer, but that answer cannot be found in the various naturalistic and behavioristic formulas with which modern man characterizes the absurdity and despair of his new-found existential condition. It cannot be found there, that is, unless modern man looks into them for the supernatural implications of the fantastic and inexplicable mysteries beneath, above, and within man's natural "compulsive instincts." As Mailer puts it: "We are all after all agents of Satan and the Lord, cause otherwise how explain the phenomenological extremities of hot shit and hurricane?" (*Vietnam*, 27–28). The gist of Mailer's intellectual challenge seems clear: there are more things in your "milieu," post-Darwinians, than are dreamt of in your determinism.

Mailer seems to have envisioned a complete cosmology based upon his resurrection of the notion that man acts as the agent of external, eternal, and omnipotent cosmic forces. They are not "Satan and the Lord" exactly, this identification being more metaphorical than anything else. But Mailer's system does appear to be analogous to the conception of the "Great Chain of Being" that dominated traditional Christian cosmology well past the Elizabethan age. Mailer seems especially aware of the psychological motivation underlying that conception. E. M. W. Tillyard in *The Elizabethan World Picture* suggests that the old-time cosmology proceeded primarily from man's fear of the cosmos, from his terrified longing for a benevolent "order" to a world he could not hope to control:

If the Elizabethans believed in an ideal order animating earthly order, they were terrified lest it should be upset, and appalled by the visible tokens of disorder that suggested its upsetting. They were obsessed by the fear of chaos and the fact of mutability; and the obsession was power-ful in proportion as their faith in the cosmic order was strong.

As a consequence of this fear, the conception of a "fixed sys-tem" that the Middle Ages and Renaissance developed from Pythagoras and Plato became not altogether separable from what Tillyard calls "the terrors of primitive superstition": "At the time when Christianity was young and growing, there was general terror of the stars and a wide practice of astrology. The terror was mainly superstitious, and the only way of miti-gating the stars' enmity was through magic." But the important point, Tillyard adds, is that "the Elizabethan believed in the pervasive operation of an external fate in the world." The ulti-mate source of man's fate was to be found in God, or the primum mobile, but Elizabethan man, harking back instinc-tively to his primitive origins, tended to locate its controlling power in the moon. In fact, the moon became the borderline between the frightening mutability that sin had subjected man to (sublunary) and the eternal immutability of the higher, more perfect spheres. And, because Elizabethans could see the "correspondences" between human events and natural phe-nomena, they could believe in their own involuntary partic-ipation in the cosmic "dance," just as their science, through observation of the tides, could comprehend, as Tillyard puts it, "the seas dancing in obedience to the moon."

Mailer's superstitions are just as primitive, but Mailer would say it is necessarily so. The truth he seeks is beyond the civi-lized intellect that has been tamed by its own sublimations; what we need to recapture, he declares in his famous essay "The White Negro," "is the sophistication of the wise primitive in a giant jungle" (317). Consequently, "magic," which some had discarded, takes its place in Mailer's scheme alongside the modern notions of "dread and the perception of death" as "the roots of motivation" (*Dream,* 15). Appropriately, Mailer's vestigial hero Rojack talks to the moon, his master; and the moon, of course, talks back (18).

Along with the powers of magic, the Elizabethans could use their science to assure themselves of not only the benevo-lence of the cosmic order but mankind's own place in it. They conceived of the physical universe, including man's body, as composed of only four elements. This insured not only the harmony of the cosmic "dance" but the necessity of human participation. As Tillyard puts it, "References to the elements in Elizabethan literature are very many and their imaginative function is to link the doings of men with the business of the cosmos, to show events not merely happening but happening in conjunction with so much else."

The naturalistic idea that "man belongs entirely in the order of nature" is not far removed from the Elizabethan idea that man is subject, like the other animals, to a universal, divinely ordained "law of nature." What differentiates the old conception and naturalistic ones is the Elizabethan's willingness to invest what Tillyard calls a "soul" in the processes of nature. This belief allowed them, moreover, to maintain a belief in their own free will even while insisting on the determinism of natural law. The "soul" of the universe was a benevolent God. Further, men believed that they too possessed souls, created in the image of God, participating in the nature of God; and, to the extent that God had free will while still obeying his own laws, man, to the limit of his imperfections, did too. They could go so far as to see man as the "microcosm" of the "macrocosm," and, as such, man was thought to contain not only the pattern of physical creation but, in Tillyard's words, the "purely rational or spiritual" essence of the primum mobile as well. But modern man seems to have lost the conception of a "dual" nature in himself. He does not ascribe to any part of his whole being an immutable essence that transcends its own mutable physical existence. Consequently, the fatality in his outlook can be explained by saying he has been forced to abdicate his deity, that he has been forced to see himself just as rigidly controlled by natural instincts and the laws of mutability as any other animal.

Mailer shares this fatalism, it seems, though his work seems also to have passed beyond the nadir of the circle (p. 35), restored a bit of mankind's majesty by granting to the instincts supernatural as well as natural power. Likewise, his only intellectual complaint about the existentialists is their ignoring the mysterious and religious in their emphasis upon the process of the sublunary physical world. As he says in "The White Negro":

To be a real existentialist (Sartre admittedly to the contrary) one must be religious, one must have one's sense of the "purpose"—whatever the purpose may be—but a life which is directed by one's faith in the necessity of action is life committed to the notion that the substratum of existence is the search, the end meaningful but mysterious; it is impossible to live such a life unless one's emotions provide their profound conviction. Only the French, alienated beyond alienation from their unconscious, could welcome an existential philosophy without ever feeling it at all. . . . [315]

The Elizabethans may not have argued for the meaningful connection between their cosmology and the "unconscious" as Mailer does, but they were wise in their time. They knew that those unseen, only felt, inner forces motivating them must be assigned a cosmic identity, "cause otherwise how explain . . . ?"

Norman Mailer, courageous enough to confront his unconscious, is now ready to admit to another idea of the nature of the universe and man's place in it. Because he knows that medieval and Elizabethan thinkers were looking into their own unconscious and not out at the stars when they saw man as the microcosm, he knows they could not be far wrong. And because he knows that the naturalistic thinkers were looking into their own unconscious and not out at the animals when they saw man in the grip of the natural instincts, he knows they could not be far wrong either. A synthesis of these different notions has certain implications. Take man's immutable soul away from him, deprive him of free will, and he becomes just another beast, an absolute slave to the laws of mutability. The thinkers of the old cosmology knew this; Tillyard states that Raleigh, for example, acknowledged that "the stars . . . had absolute sway over plants and beasts." This is old wisdom. However, if one admits of man's animal nature and still insists on man as the microcosm, he puts the old wisdom into a new perspective. Man, the microcosm, contains within his nature the transcending link between the process and the power, between physical reality and the laws that transcend and control it. The old thinkers looked for the mirror image of this transcendent power within the human mind. But when spirit and free will are denied to man they must be denied to the "soul" of the universe also. Now when modern man looks into his unconscious for the power that transcends it, he will see the mirror image of his animal body: "The lights were saying that there was something up here, and it was really here, yeah God was here, and He was real and no man was He, but a beast, some beast of a giant jaw and cavernous mouth with a full cave's breath and fangs, and secret call: come to me" (*Vietnam,* 217).

There is never any question of free will in Mailer's depiction of the actions of his hero/narrators Rojack and D. J.; they act by unreasoned impulse, and all their reflections are after the fact. Like the salmon's homing impulse, the unconscious urges that give direction to their actions transcend their individual intelligences. But the irony beyond irony that Mailer is suggesting is that since God is a beast, he can have no free will either. He is as rigidly mechanistic as the homing instinct, which, in turn, has no free will in the teeth of the law of mutability (the birth-death cycle) that its intricate psychological machinery serves. God has no choice but to call man to Himself, just as the bear that Tex and D. J. study in the wilderness has no choice but to eat the caribou it has chased and killed (*Vietnam,* 206–7): it is all an integral part of the cycle. This scene in the wilderness closely resembles that in William Faulkner's story "The Bear." Tex and D. J. bury their guns and packs (187) in a cache, just as the young boy in Faulkner's story got rid of "the watch, the compass, the stick—the three lifeless mechanicals." In both cases it is an act of "integration" (to return to Koestler's term), an attempt in both cases to rid themselves of the compulsion to master nature and to synchronize, instead, their individual wills with nature's patterns. The "center of things" may be "insane with force" as D. J. suggests (151), a system of cycles within cycles, compulsions beyond compulsions; but man's attempts to break into the integral cycles with such lifeless mechanicals as high-powered rifles, compasses, and even helicopters seem to Mailer pathetic efforts to reestablish human free will in the presence of an infinitely finer madness.

Insanity is the ultimate nature of the universe because the

machinery is in control; the hammer swings the arm. The old-
time thinkers, looking deep within the unconscious, sensed
this, and with the analogical light of astrology they were able to
project a vision of it into the heavens (using the term "projection" in the sense of both Freud and book 7 of Plato's
Republic). Because they could feel the machinery in motion,
they could conceive of the universe as a harmonious "dance";
and, because they could feel their own participation in the
dance, they knew the dancing partner of the stars, according
to Tillyard, must be "Fate." What is fascinating to a modern
thinker like Mailer is that the old conception of the universe
as a "dance" almost perfectly parallels the picture that Albert
Einstein's Unified Field Theory provides. And, if the Elizabethans were right about the dance of the stars, could they
also have been right about their dancing partner?

Einstein, according to Lincoln Barnett in *The Universe and
Dr. Einstein,* pondered the apparent division of the universe
into matter and energy, and he decided that they are one,
dissimilar only in temporary state. Thus, the elemental building blocks of nature are more inseparable than any Elizabethan
theory of the elements could have envisioned. Further, Einstein decided that the motions of electricity and of magnetism
cannot ultimately be differentiated, that neither can gravity
and inertia, nor gravity and any of the others (one does not
have to be a mathematician to appreciate the significance of
the "coincidence" that Newton's mathematical expression of
the law of gravity, $F = Gmm^1/d^2$, is essentially the same as the
formula for the force of attraction between two unlike electrical
charges, $F = Cqq^1/d^2$, and as that for the force of attraction
between two unlike magnetic poles, $F = K\,MM^1/d^2$). Motion,
in fact, turns out to be the underlying reality of the universe.
According to the modern theory, then, the bodies of the universe do move in a "dance," one as unified and harmonious as
any of the Elizabethan astrologers imagined. The old science
located the cause of the motion in the force that each body
exerts on other bodies. But now Einstein discovers that motion
is not caused by force; motion just is; it is the acausal ordering
principle of the dance. As Lincoln Barnett explains it,

Einstein's Law of Gravitation contains nothing about force. It describes the behavior of objects in a gravitational field—the planets, for example—not in terms of 'attraction' but simply in terms of the paths they follow. To Einstein, gravitation is simply part of inertia: the movements of the stars and the planets stem from their inherent inertia.

Every body, big and little, moves in concert with other bodies, and as they move gravitational and electromagnetic fields develop that define the tempo, spin, or direction of any given body. "And, underlying all the harmonious movement of the universe, there is a deeper reality," in Barnett's words, "a basic universal field within which gravitational and electromagnetic fields are merely particular ephemeral forms or conditions of state." Motion, the machination of the universe, is in control. Insane, but in this conception, Barnett suggests, rests the hope of reintegration between microcosm and macrocosm, of parts to the whole, that the old Chain of Being promised:

Whether the whole grand objective of a Unified Theory will be realized only many more . . . years of mathematical and experimental work can determine. But in its vast cosmic picture, when fully revealed, the abyss between macrocosmic and microcosmic—the very big and the very little —will surely be bridged, and the whole complex of the universe will resolve into a homogeneous fabric in which matter from the slow wheeling of the galaxies to the wild flight of electrons become simply changes in the structure and concentrations of the primordial field.

Just as the thinkers of the old cosmology used their science to explain man's link to the nature of the universe, Mailer uses modern science to examine the nature of the "deeper reality" as it operates in man. Modern mathematics cannot say why its laws work; it cannot even suggest how they work; it can only describe what happens when they work. Similarly, Mailer does not concern himself with the why or how of the "deeper reality" that the old thinkers identified as "Satan and the Lord." He only attempts to describe the *what* of its shifting "structure and concentrations." It seems that the "God" he is describing is somehow the manifestation of the "primordial field," and that this universal law of motion is what the microcosm, any particular human being, participates in when he transcends his physical limitations to experience the essence of God's power. In "The White Negro" Mailer goes so far as to suggest that maybe, just maybe, by tuning into motion, a man can capture a little of the deifying free will that the old cosmology promised at "the center of things": "In motion a man has a chance, his body is warm, his instincts are quick, and when the crisis comes, whether of love or violence, he can make it, he can win, he can release a little more energy for himself. . . ." (323).

Rojack can receive his vision of that "heaven" on "the other side of the door" only at the climax of the periods of the purest, least reflective, most self-perpetuating, most godlike, motion: at a time of "violence" when he murders Deborah (*Dream*, 35) and at a time of "love" when he creates an embryo with Cherry (122). Mailer must be thinking of that sensation we all have had, in a moment of intense emotions or danger, that time is suspended in a slow, graceful, often terrifying dance in which wholes seem to separate in a slow dissolve into discernible parts and the parts to coalesce back into rounder wholes, when in reality our body rate has speeded up and events are clashing upon one another in the rapid succession of the moment. Perhaps Mailer is suggesting a psychic analogue (p. 29) to Einstein's theory that as matter is propelled at speeds approaching the speed of light, its relative time slows down until perhaps, at the ultimate speed, time stops altogether. Perhaps, if there is such an analogue, man could still achieve some kind of immortality or salvation (see p. 89; see also Plato's *Phaedrus*, "that which is ever in motion is immortal"). In any case, Rojack wins his own salvation but seems something less than godlike in doing it. Facing Kelly's challenge to walk the parapet, Rojack knows from where he will have to draw his power: "I had to keep moving, everything was getting worse the longer I stayed still, but my feet were bad again" (242). He walks the parapet once for himself; the voice of God tells him he will have to walk it again for Cherry; but he loses his godlike momentum and hence his courage; Cherry dies. He has a chance to win her on the parapet, in the deifying movement of the present, but his mind drifts between the dead past and the uncreated future where nothing ever moves.

Mailer may have begun with the intention of making Rojack a tragic hero of the new cosmological order, as Lear and Hamlet were tragic heroes caught in the process of the old order. But it takes a certain amount of old-fashioned romanticism to take that kind of tragedy seriously, a certain sense of the cause-and-effect that ties the individual act to its cosmic repercussions (pp. 47–48). So Mailer's heroes, Rojack and D. J., win no glorious victories and suffer no final defeats; but they do learn to live like animals after they become alienated from their corrupt society, living each day, as Mailer in *Of a Fire on the Moon* says of the Hemingway brand of heroism, "next to the breath of the beast," accepting their "portion of dread every day"; and though less than willing, they are "ready," always ready, "to share the dread of the Lord."

D. J. appears to be the adolescent counterpart of the hipster "psychopath" that Mailer describes in "The White Negro" (who seems roughly equivalent, in turn, to Ellison's Rinehart). This is the individual whose instincts are as sharp as an animal's because his fast life of perpetual danger, drugs, and existential despair has forced him to live, as the animals must, within the unsafe "groove" or "motion" of the present; unlike the civilized, socialized man whose peaceful, reflective existence allows him to escape into the mental world of the past and future—far from the essence and "dread" of the Lord. D. J.'s use of scatalogical language can be explained as the result of the hipster's intense experience of God in the motion of the present. He understands the animalism of the "deeper reality" underlying our existential condition and needs a holy language adequately to express it:

. . . it is not too difficult to believe that the language of Hip which evolved was an artful language, tested and shaped by intense experience and therefore different in kind from white slang, as different as the special obscenity of the soldier, which in its emphasis upon "ass" as the soul and "shit" as circumstance, was able to express the existential states of the enlisted man. [*Negro*, 322]

Most significant, as the language of the hipster reaches down to express the purely animal processes of man's existence, it cannot do otherwise than reach out to embrace the nature of the "primordial field" underlying the universe, because man is, after all, the microcosm:

> It is a pictorial language. . . . imbued with the dialectic of small but intense change, a language for the microcosm, in this case, man, for it takes the immediate experiences of any passing man and magnifies the dynamic of his movements, not specifically but abstractly so that he is seen more as a vector in a network of forces than as a static character in a crystal-lized field. [*Negro*, 322]

What Mailer says of hipster language Richard Poirier in *Norman Mailer* observes in Mailer's own language, indicating again (pp. 44–45) the centrality of metaphysics to the visionary writer's art:

> Mailer's style, very much in Faulkner's mode, keeps everything in *motion;* everything contends with, joins, is infused with everything else. . . . Mailer's fondness for participles—"going," "fading," "settling," "silvering"— expresses his taste for actions that go on simultaneously, for a kind of bombardment of impressions, registered also in his repetitions of phrase, the echoing of sound, and the use of negatives which caution against fixing the picture in any familiar frame ("September light not fading, no, ebbing"). These habits, again as in Faulkner, are consistent with a tendency to collapse the rational insistence on distinctions between time and place, so that most get measured by the seasons, and between the presumably assigned functions of the senses, so that by a synesthesia of light and sound it can be suggested that the landscape sends out and receives signals. Nature, it would seem, has its own communications system without any need for technological assistance. . . . [my italics]

Lear could see a correspondence between his inner emotions and the outer phenomena of the storm because he was sure of his own microcosmic identity and participation, therefore, in the workings of the macrocosm. D. J. holds a similar belief, only this time unification is from the side of matter rather than spirit. For D. J. the ass is literally the soul and shit is circum-stance. Since God is bestial, not spiritual, D. J. conceptualizes the divine creative act in sexual terms. The macrocosmic penis, he tells us, has been "slipping right into us," into the "bowels of creation" (*Vietnam,* 24), our collective anus. It has conceived "DNA/RNA," the embryo of our all-determining instincts, and mankind is off like a "vector" in a field of force.

Just as God has slipped his essence into man, that "electromagnetic field called earth" is the result of the principle of motion penetrating the earth at its North and/or South Pole "orifice" (*Vietnam,* 168). Thus, nature's "communications system" is "without any need for technological assistance" because its own electromagnetic, sexual circuits are infinitely more refined than any man can create artificially. Mailer has told Laura Adams in an interview for *Partisan Review* that in *Why Are We in Vietnam?* he trusted the powers of "metaphor" to lead him to "yet to be discovered" scientific truths about the connection between electromagnetism and such an organic phenomenon as, for example, the "pine sap in a tree." This is no longer a matter strictly of speculation; science writer David M. Rorvik in an article for *Esquire* "Do the French Have a Cure for Cancer?" reports that "there is quite a lot of evidence to suggest that magnetic fields have profound effects on biological organisms," apparently through interaction with the electrically charged atoms called ions that exist within the cells. The most dramatic evidence to date is a powerful electromagnetic device invented by Antoine Prioré which apparently "cures" diseases like cancer "by stimulating the biological defense mechanisms of the organism." So far, according to Rorvik, the most sophisticated attempts by sceptical scentists to prove the machine a fraud have failed.

Now we not only have a naturalistic basis for explaining the "correspondence" of the powers of the earth to those within man but a rationale for D. J.'s insistence that these powers are more intense near the North Pole. D. J. and Tex long to be "tuned in" (57) like the animals that live near the magnetically intense pole. And as they leave the human concerns and confusions of the hunting party behind, D. J. can feel it happening:

...we are going back to Aurora Borealis cause it is the only mountain of heavenly light which is certified to be result and product of magnetic disturbances—dig! you long patient asshole, we are on the track of something—that early morning chill is tuning the boys up because they getting the stone ice telepathic hollow from the bowels of the earth after it passed through the magnetic North Pole orifice. [169]

But this is not simple pastoralism; it is pastoralism sharpened by the knowledge that "animal murder is near" (193), that "the odor died last of all" (208) is this "wounded heart of things" (212). And D. J. always brings the pastoral issue back to its sexual roots, because, as we are no longer prepared to doubt, murder is a sexual act and sex is an act of murder (see the quotation from Freud, pp. 71–72), and both are connected to the unseen circuits of the dark:

... and once again they feel just as clean and on-edge and perfect as would you, sedentary send-in-terror auditor of this trip, when you, sir, are about to insert the best piece of cock you ever mustered up into a cunt which is all fuck for you, and your noze is ozone you so clean and perfect, well, they feeling like that every instant now, whoo-ee! whoo-ee; they can hardly hold it in, cause this mother nature is as big and dangerous and mysterious as a beautiful castrating cunt when she's on the edge between murder and love. . . . [197]

The thinkers of the old cosmology explained the sympathetic harmony of man and nature in a scientific "language for the microcosm" that compared the four humours in man to the four elements of nature. Mailer's parallel language turns the physics of relativity and field theory into a metaphysical vision of the laws of motion controlling human behavior just as surely and mysteriously as they do the movement of an iron filing, planet, sun, or galaxy through whatever electromagnetic fields determine their respective fates:

... where you going when you sleep? Well, hole, there's only one place you go, and that's into the undiscovered magnetic-electro fief of the dream [undiscovered as yet, but postulated also by Arthur Koestler; "the psycho-magnetic field," see p. 32], which is opposed to the electromagnetic field of the earth just as properly as the square root of minus one is opposed to one. Right! They never figured out yet whether light is wave, corpuscle, or hung up on finding her own identity [p. 26], all they know once you get down to it is that light is bright, and therefore not necessarily opposed to being part of the Universal Mind [this seems equivalent to

Barnett's "primordial field"] .... Clem—you can't get fucked for less—here is the sweet underground poop: when you go into sleep, that mind of yours leaps, stirs, and sifts itself into the Magnetic-Electro fief of the dream, . . . you are a part of the spook flux of the night like an iron filing in the E. M. field [as in the perennial high school science experiment] . . . and it all flows, mind and asshole, anode and cathode, you sending messages and receiving all through the night. . . . [*Vietnam*, 180]

And Rojack too can sense this universal mind or primordial field grooving the path of his own intense odyssey; he can feel it most intensely when he is exactly "on the edge between murder and love": "There was a presence in the room like the command of a dead pharaoh. . . . Even as a magnet directs every iron particle in a crowd of filings, so a field of force was on me here. . . . That same field of force had come on me as I left Deborah's body on the floor and started down the stairs to the room where Ruta was waiting" (*Dream*, 44, 220).

But if man is fully to comprehend "the phenomenological extremities" of the "hot shit" of his microcosmic self and the "hurricane" of the natural correspondence, he must now be willing to understand that any electromagnetic field has within itself the capability of restructure, of reversal:

". . . just no chance, know this, you are a part of the dream field, you the square root of minus one, you off in a flux, part of a circuit, you swinging on the inside of a deep mystery, which is whatever is electricity and who is magnetism. . . . Magnetism potential and electricity actual of the Prince himself? . . . the electricity and magnetism of the dream field is reversed—God or the Devil takes over in sleep—what simpler explanation you got . . .? [*Vietnam*, 182)

Mailer, like Melville, confronts the problem of the duality of nature (p. 65), finding it to be a manifestation of the primordial field's being "hung up on finding her own identity." Rojack's sexual encounter with Ruta, for example, during which Rojack alternates between her anus and her vagina, characterized by Rojack as "a raid on the devil and a trip back to the Lord" (*Dream*, 48), has prompted some critics to say that Rojack is selling his soul to the Devil in this scene. Mailer has called himself a Manichean so many times that the temptation is to see this sort of scene in old-fashioned, and romantic, cause-and-effect terms. Rojack has no "choice" to make here, like the one Max F. Schulz has suggested in "Mailer's Divine Comedy," but is merely following, as he says, "a command from inside of me." His actions are determined by how the primordial field is defining itself, whether as the Devil or as the Lord, at any given time; his will goes no further than the conflicting "series of orders" which travel like "whiplike tracers of light" (*Dream*, 35) from head to body and back again.

At the moment when an animal is "on the edge between murder and love" the primordial field sends the message out, electricity activates the magnetic field, and God *or* the Devil takes over:

So they breathed hard with all of this, lying next to each other like two rods getting charged with magnetism in electric coils. . . . They could almost have got up and walked across the pond and into the north without their boots, going up to disappear and die and join that great beast. In the field of all such desire D. J. raised his hand to put it square on Tex's cock and squeeze and just before he did the Northern lights shifted on that moment and a coil of sound went off in the night like a blowout in some circuit of the structure of the dark . . . now it was there, murder between them under all friendship, for God was a beast, not a man, and God said, "Go out and kill—fulfill my will, go and kill," and they hung there on the knife of the divide in all conflict of lust to own the other . . . and they were twins, never to be as near as lovers again, but killer brothers, owned by something, prince of darkness, lord of light, they did not know; they just knew that telepathy was on them. . . . [*Vietnam*, 216, 217-18, 219]

The thinkers of the old cosmology were willing to admit of the possibility that mankind is "owned by something" but only so long as their rationalism and science would allow them to assume the all-powerful benevolence of their owner. But modern existentialists, as Mailer has suggested to Laura Adams, are obsessed with the suspicion that "nothing is nailed down" any more; either God cannot control everything or God Himself is subject to the 180° swings in mood that any animal trainer can testify make wild animals as "dangerous and mysterious" to work with "as a beautiful castrating cunt when she's on the edge between murder and love." Mailer seems to understand that precisely because the old-time thinkers felt secure they could afford to take a fairly accurate analogical picture of the connection between their inner natures and the design of the cosmos. Likewise, he seems suspicious of the modern thinker's haste to explain away or ignore the mysterious, seemingly supernatural forces operating within him. Existential man, in his quest for self-determination and self-exaltation, can afford to admit the power of the degrading but still manageable animal instincts but cannot afford to admit that the power of those instincts demands as much reverence as Yahweh, the ancient God of dread Whose name one dared not utter. So Mailer's cosmology provides not merely an evocative "dream allegory" (p. 44) but a metaphorical system paying the deepest respect to the truth at the "center of things."

9

DICKEY'S AMERICAN EPIC

Leonard Lutwack, in *Heroic Fiction,* has stated that Melville's *Moby-Dick* introduced "unequivocally the spirit of the epic to American fiction by daring to endow native materials with qualities of the heroic past." Lutwack's book attempts to make clear just what those qualities are and what American variations we can expect on the ancient forms and themes. James Dickey's *Deliverance* needs a similar critical approach because it fits the ancient pattern more closely than any of the novels Lutwack chooses to discuss (it seems, in fact, an almost perfect embodiment of Joseph Campbell's "monomyth"). And *Deliverance,* therefore, might represent the approach of American fiction to the zenith of Frye's modal cycle (p. 46), a goal toward which it has been heading since the days of Poe and Melville.

"The dominant tendency of the American epic novel," according to Lutwack,

is the deliberate return to primitive motifs: the prowess of warriors in Cooper and Simms, the revenge against a monster in *Moby-Dick,* the battle to the death in *The Octopus* and *For Whom the Bell Tolls,* the migration of a people in *The Grapes of Wrath.* No American epic hero

---

Parenthetical pagination in this chapter refers to *Deliverance* (Boston: Houghton, 1970).

fights to save a city, as is so common in the Renaissance epic, but always to preserve some less sophisticated way of life.

The American epic novel, then, represents a return to what C. S. Lewis in *A Preface to Paradise Lost* calls "The Primary Epic," the kind of epic that Homer wrote or *Beowulf* is, as opposed to "The Secondary Epic" that the Renaissance inherited from Virgil (Lewis's distinction suggests that Homer's epics belong to the romance, not high mimetic, mode). "The qualities of the heroic past" that Lutwack says inform our greatest fiction have nothing to do with the "great national subject" that since Virgil has been associated with the epic. Lewis:

> The truth is that Primary Epic neither had, nor could have, a great subject in the later sense. That kind of greatness arises only when some event can be held to effect a profound and more or less permanent change in the history of the world, as the founding of Rome did, or still more, the fall of man [as in *Paradise Lost*]. Before any event can have significance, history must have some degree of pattern, some design. The mere endless up and down, the constant aimless alternations of glory and misery, which make up the terrible phenomenon called a Heroic Age, admit no such design. No one event is really very much more important than another. No achievement can be permanent: today we kill and feast, tomorrow we are killed, and our women led away as slaves. Nothing "stays put," nothing has a significance beyond the moment. Heroism and tragedy there are in plenty, therefore good stories in plenty; but no "large design that brings the world out of the good to ill." The total effect is not a pattern, but a kaleidoscope. If Troy falls, woe to the Trojans, no doubt, but what of it? "Zeus has loosened the heads of many cities, and many more will he loosen yet" (*Il.* IX). . . . It is all the more terrible because the poet takes it all for granted, makes no complaint.

In a time when the suspicion begins to grow, as Mailer puts it, that "nothing is nailed down" or, as Lewis puts it, that "nothing 'stays put,'" Dickey would take us back across time to the time before man had a sense of history but did, instead, take "for granted" his place in the natural cycle of birth and death. The country people in *Deliverance* seem grotesque and simple-minded to city people like Bobby, Drew, and Ed, but Lewis Medlock tells Ed that "we're lesser men" (57) than they, because they live the kind of natural existence that city-bound men have lost over the civilized centuries.

Lewis Medlock is cut from the mold of the "primitive" epic hero, the champion of a "less sophisticated way of life" who is as ready to "plunge outside of history" as Ellison's Tod Clifton. As Odysseus was the man "never at a loss," Lewis is, according to the narrator Ed Gentry, "the only man I knew who could do with his life exactly what he wanted to" (15). "He was not only self-determined; he was determined." The obligatory epic description of his "prowess" reads: "He was one of the best tournament archers in the state and, even at the age of thirty-eight or -nine, one of the strongest men I had ever shaken hands with" (16). Ed Gentry, the quintessential contemporary American, a soft and overweight suburbanite, finds himself nonetheless "of the chosen" (46) of Lewis. If this is not exactly the honor of being chosen by Odysseus to man the voyage to Ithaca, it is at least as good as being asked by Papa himself to join him on the "tragic adventure" of fishing the swamp on the big two-hearted river. And since Lewis's river happens to flow through just such a dreaded underworld, his weekend canoe trip takes on an epical significance demanding an American-bred heroism that is at least Hemingwayesque, if not Homeric.

The tragedies and triumphs of Homeric epic, according to C. S. Lewis, were played against a "background of meaningless flux," played against the sense of the "permanence, the *indifference,* the heartrending or consoling fact that whether we laugh or weep the world is what it is" (my italics). In other words, there were no cosmic implications to the epic hero's actions; the indifferent, often malicious, though usually simply capricious, gods assigned no ultimate rewards for his good acts or eternal damnation for his errors, as would be the fate of the heroes of Christian epics of later centuries. The action of *Deliverance* is played against the Homeric background. As Ed says in a moment of revelation during his climb up the side of the cliff, "The river was blank and mindless with beauty. . . . I beheld the river in its icy pit of brightness, in its far-below sound and *indifference,* in its large coil and tiny points and flashes of moon, in its long sinuous form, in its uncomprehending consequence" (177, my italics). The experience of *Deliverance* is a return in time (symbolized by the line Ed describes between the urban South and rural South, 48) to a pre-Christian era to match that of our "post-Christian America" (Saul Bellow's phrase, *Herzog*), a return to a time much like our own when values were grabbed on the run and meaning was where you found it, to a time when the hero's role was not diminished by the indifference of the cosmos to his actions but heightened thereby because heroism was *all*. The final difference between meaning and meaninglessness was the hero's ability, versus his inability, to act when the necessary time came (Mailer's "existential edge"). This is the nature of Ed's discovery after undergoing an initiation rite into heroism on the death climb up the cliff: in an indifferent universe governed by no laws except natural forces (the metaphor of which Ed sees in the running of the river, 176), "Who knows what might not be possible?" (178). All things heroic seem possible to the man who can liberate himself from the ties of a too-easy civilization and make himself ready to start with the cosmic blankness that was all Odysseus had to work with: "I think," says Lewis, "the machines are going to fail, the political systems are going to fail, and a few men are going to take to the hills and start over" (51).

Jay Gatsby, Fitzgerald wrote, not without irony, "sprang from his Platonic conception of himself." Fitzgerald saw this same vestige of romantic individualism in Hemingway, the same passion for self-exaltation as the only bulwark against the void, nada. The place to start when post-Christian man starts over, it seems, will be with the self; every man his own messiah, his own epic hero. "We are what we pretend to be," Kurt Vonnegut has said with a shudder, but in this final irreducible irony, a Hemingwayesque hero like Lewis finds the hope of deliverance: "It depends on how strong your fantasy is, and whether you really—*really*—in your own mind, fit into your fantasy, whether you measure up to what you've fantasized" (59).

Lewis, like Jay Gatsby, walks the thin line between the ridiculous and the sublime, and Lewis is as much an enigma to Ed as Gatsby is to Nick. Ed, like Nick, has the hero role thrust upon him when his own Odysseus falls wounded. This marks a significant American departure from the classical norm.

It would have been inconceivable, for example, for Homer to allow Odysseus to fall victim to an enemy as formidable as the Cyclops, for then the mantle of heroism would be thrust onto the shoulders of one of the nondescript members of Odysseus' crew. But Dickey is writing for the ironic age, an age so beyond inspiration that what is needed is not greater heroes but that every individual, in the spirit of Jacksonian democracy, rise to the demands of his inborn potential for heroism. This is what Lutwack calls "the democratization of the epic hero's attributes," pointing out that the hero of the American epic is most often "an apprentice-hero, rather like Telemachus than Roland, who has latent heroic energy and must learn the cause he is willing to serve and the manner in which he must serve it."

Thus, *Deliverance* is something other than just an epic; it is a *Bildungsroman,* a novel of Ed Gentry's education, playing Telemachus to Lewis's Odysseus, in the mysteries of heroism. Ed begins by being amused by Lewis's atavistic faith in the body as the ultimate source of human survival:

> "I know," he [Lewis] said. "You think I'm some kind of narcissistic fanatic. But I'm not."
> "I wouldn't put it that way, exactly," I said.
> "I just believe," he said, "that the whole thing is going to be reduced to the human body, once and for all. I want to be ready."
> "*What* whole thing?"
> "The human race thing." [51]

In a cerebral society in which all bodily functions have been reduced to a complex of sublimations, and a dominant male threatens other submissive males with transfer to the branch office in Juneau rather than with physical harm, vanity is perhaps the principal reason a man can have for developing his muscles. But while society may nurture narcissism (pp. 67–69), the wilderness teaches humility; a man of the wilderness develops his body as a hedge against its proven vulnerability. As Lewis says of the time he broke his ankle going up a cliff while alone in the forest, "The old human body is the same as it always was. It still feels that old fear, and that old pain" (60). And after Ed experiences the primordial feelings of fear and pain on another cliff in the same wilderness, he discovers that his own deliverance will depend on his making Lewis's mystique of the body work for himself: "I wanted to kill him [the evil mountain man] exactly as Lewis had killed the other man" (180).

Hemingway dead by his own hand, Gatsby the victim of the "foul dust" of industrial society that "floated in the wake of his dreams"; these are the real-life and fictional embodiments of the American frontier spirit, reverse-scapegoats fighting not for the chance to "light out for the territory" but against the social mechanisms that threaten to cut off the individual from his last lingering sense of source. As Lewis teaches Ed, a man must never let his social role obscure his natural identity:

"You've been sitting in a chair that won't move. You've been steady. But when the river is under you, all that is going to change. There's nothing you do as vice-president of Emerson-Gentry that's going to make any difference at all, when the water starts to foam up. Then, it's not going to be what your title says you do, but what you end up doing. You know: *doing.*" [51]

Some critics have wondered about the necessity for the long accounts of the activities of Ed and his companions before they reach the wilderness river and after they leave it, and the movie version cuts them altogether. But Dickey probably wanted to dramatize the difference between what Campbell calls in *The Hero with a Thousand Faces* the "region of supernatural wonder" and "the world of common day," the difference between the deep wilderness, where "bare survival" (53) is the highest moral value and the identities of hero and scapegoat are elementarily defined, and the world of law and convention (for which Drew and the sheriff serve as spokesmen), where the dead are dug up so that dams can be built to flood the wilderness (272) and the hero can expect to be made a scapegoat (the sheriff to Ed: "Don't come back up here," 270).

The contrast is as disorienting to Ed as it appears to have been for many of Dickey's critics. As his mind struggles to comprehend the unreal reality he is suddenly caught in, Ed identifies the larger than life dramatics of his situation with the kind of epic that a contemporary American knows best:

From where we were the cliff looked something like a gigantic drive-in movie screen waiting for an epic film to begin. I listened for interim music, glancing now and again up the pale curved stone for Victor Mature's stupendous image, wondering where it would appear, or if the whole thing were not now already playing, and I hadn't yet managed to put it together. . . . "I think he means to pick the rest of us off tomorrow," I said out loud, still stranger than anything I had ever imagined. "When do the movies start, Lord?" [154, 157]

Dickey has been accused by some reviewers of designing his novel according to its suitability for adaptation for the movies, but there is something in Dickey's self-conscious use of the "movies" motif that suggests this is not so dishonest a motivation as some critics like to make it appear. Perhaps Dickey sees in the popular art form something of the larger than common-day-life aura that is the essence of our archetypal fantasies. If he does, he is in agreement with the thesis of James Mellard's recent book *Four Modes.* Mellard theorizes that there are essentially four ways of telling a story: the oral formulaic, the pictorial, the dramatic, and the lyrical. The "order in which the modes developed is essentially congruent with the historical development of fiction." The oral formulaic reflects in part the repetitiveness necessary for oral presentation to an unsophisticated audience, but its heavy emphasis on recurrent *"topoi"* and *"mythoi"* suggests also its natural position near the mythic zenith of the modal cycle, where, according to Frye's "Theory of Myths," we expect to find "the structural principles of literature isolated." The development of the other modes, which display rather more feeling for the texture of life than for its structure, has seemed for the most part dependent on external influences such as "discoveries in the other arts," "new ideas in philosophy," and scientific developments. The dramatic and lyrical modes are strictly modern developments that seem most dependent on discoveries in depth psychology and theoretical science. As modern man becomes more and more convinced of the relativity and subjectivity of the individual point of view, he either struggles to make his story as true to the "external, observable fact" as possible (the dramatic mode) or he abandons the attempt to synthesize external reality to pursue "internal, mental" phenomena (the lyrical mode). But through it all Mellard sees the ancient formulas of narrative structure, *"mythoi,"* surviving, and surviving because they fulfil "recurrent" human needs. They survive in all fiction but they thrive, according to Mellard, in the popular art forms such as detective novels and Western movies, exoskeletal narratives written for unsophisticated audiences, in fact, the same melodramatic fictions that Frye identifies with the ironic comic mode. It could be that what Mellard calls the pictorial, dramatic, and lyrical are species of the "displacement" that Frye says the natural "rhythm, or recurrent movement" of literature undergoes as our changing perceptions balance the recurrent human needs with the growing need to tell "a credible or plausible story" (pp. 35–37). And it could be that, now that we have gone as far in the direction of psychological reductionism as the lyrical mode will take us, the next logical step is a return, as Frye has predicted, to the primordial *mythoi* that are "deeply founded on the natural cycle." If this synthesis of Frye's and Mellard's interpretations of the "historical development of fiction" is tenable, the current critical fascination with "popular literature," and the subsequent lionization of such figures as Dashiell Hammett and Alfred Hitchcock, would seem more than just a fad, and Dickey's "popular" novel, as satisfying to the masses as a "good flick," might deserve serious attention as to its view of just what the recurrent human needs are and how they can be fulfilled in the presence of this now civilized continent. The question once again is: "How to be!"

The would-be contemporary American epic hero must learn first of all that his own life can have epic or mythic implications, but only if he bears the responsibility for his own deliverance that he would rather leave on the stronger shoulders of Odysseus, Victor Mature, or Lewis Medlock: "The assurance with which he had killed a man was desperately frightening to me," Ed says of Lewis, "but the same quality was also calming, and I moved, without being completely aware of movement, nearer to him. I would have liked nothing better than to touch that big relaxed forearm.... I would have followed him anywhere...." (135). Now Ed finds himself miscast as the epic hero in a classically defined kill-or-be-killed confrontation, and the thought makes his "tongue thicken at the possibility" (189).

Dickey uses archery to dramatize, and symbolize, the epic struggle of mind to master matter and of will to master fear. The arrow becomes the extension of the hero's will, and the rightness of its flight to the target mirrors the straightness of the archer's mind. As Ed remarks, "There is no skill or sport, not even surgery or golf, in which confidence is as important as it is in archery" (195). And as he approaches the test of his own epic stature, to settle the question of killing or being killed, he declares, "I knew that my next battle would be with hysteria, the wild hysteria of full draw, of wanting to let the arrow go and get the tension of holding the bow out of the body; to get the shot off and get it over with" (195–96). And a little later he adds, "I was full of the transfiguring power of the full draw, the draw hysteria that is the ruination of some archers and the making of others, who can conquer it and make it work for them" (197). The archery shot becomes the perfect test of the epic hero, as it was for Odysseus when he returned to challenge the suitors. The question is: Will he hit what he is aiming at? Will the hero have the grace under pressure of death, if he misses, not to miss?

Lewis stands at full draw for a full minute, a demanding situation for an archer because the steadiness of his aim ebbs away with his strength, waiting for the right moment to shoot the man holding the shotgun on Ed. The man, of course, is "center shot." We expect this steadiness and psychological "cool" from Lewis, as the ancients expected it from Odysseus, who made his incredible shot through the axe heads, Homer tells us, having never bothered to get up from his banquet seat. But we do not know what to expect from Ed, the "dumb brute" common man, when his time comes. This is the essence of the American epic: Will the common man, given his opportunity for deliverance, be able to conquer the hysteria that stalks us all? The reader is apprehensive because earlier Ed had "exploded . . . high and wide" (106) when he tried to shoot a deer. With this scene in mind, the reader waits for Ed's resolve to fail. It does, at his first glimpse of the mountain man, and pity and fear flood the hearts of all those readers in suburbia who suspect the same deeply rooted cowardice in themselves:

This is it, I thought, but my first thought, one I could not keep off me, was that I could stay in the tree until he went away. My climb up the cliff had left me; all I wanted was my life. Everything in me was shaking; I could not even have notched the arrow. [194]

Ed has set himself up for a shot reminiscent of that of Odysseus. He is sitting in a pine tree where he makes an "alley-way of needles" like Odysseus' alley-way of axe heads. But the startling intimacy or oneness that this creates between himself and his target triggers an internal crisis to which heroes like Lewis and Odysseus never seem susceptible: "The whole careful structure of my shot began to come apart, and I struggled in my muscles and guts and heart to hold it together" (197). We can identify so strongly with Ed's susceptibility to such panic, perhaps, because we so strongly want to identify with Lewis's insusceptibility to it. But where does the contemporary American everyman, suddenly caught in a cyclone of danger, helplessly wavering between control and hysteria, find the spiritual stuff to hold himself together?

The mythic hero and the epic hero seem naturally though mysteriously to hold their "muscles and guts and heart" together, but what is the source of such inner resonance? Dickey suggests an answer in his poem "Winter Trout"; the protagonist, who is bow fishing, takes aim on a trout,

> With a shot like Ulysses'
> Through the ax heads, with the great weapon.

Somehow the perfect shot goes wrong. He interprets it

> As a sign of the penalties
> For breaking into closed worlds
>
> Where the wary controllers lie
> At the heart of their power,
> A pure void of shadowy purpose
> Where the gods live, attuning the world.

The archer here is not in balance with the forces that attune natural existence, whereas the trout is (p. 123); the evasive move of the trout is instinctively right, while the shot is merely technically correct. And as Lewis teaches Ed, archery that is "not purely instinctive" is not really archery (39). This lesson in archery provides an explanation for the inaccuracy of Ed's shot at the deer and, if we can believe he has sharpened his instincts somewhere along the way, the accuracy of his shot at the mountain man. The explanation is part of Lewis's encompassing code for living, his mystique of the body as the source of deliverance. He tells Ed that in the hills, far from the noisy unreality of the city,

"You could make a kind of life that wasn't out of touch with the other forms of life. Where the seasons would mean something, would mean everything [see the quotation from Frye, p. 36]. Where you could hunt as you needed to, and maybe do a little light farming, and get along. You'd die early, and you'd suffer, but you'd be in touch." [54]

Dickey's use of the archery shot as the symbol and dramatization of the hero's balance of body and mind, instinct and intellect, that signals his resonance with the forces of nature is reminiscent of another American contribution to the mystique of epic heroism, that of Fenimore Cooper's frontier scout, Natty Bumppo. In *The Pioneers* (1823) we find Natty involved in a turkey shoot with a local hero named Billy Kirby. Billy, given credit for "steady nerves and quick eye," is an even favorite to beat Natty. But Natty kills the elusive turkey, while boasting, "I'll show you a man who's made better shots afore now, and that when he's been hard pressed by the savages and wild beasts." He is the walking proof that there is more to straight shooting than steady nerves and a good eye, that the heart has to be right for the shot to be right, that God punishes the man who puts the gun to his shoulder with evil intent. Later in the novel, when he comes upon Billy and his friends wantonly shooting at a flock of pigeons, he warns them that, though they may "waste" nature with their buckshot, they will never have the "true aim" necessary to survive in the wilderness. To prove his point, when they challenge him, he brings down a distant pigeon with a single ball, an impossible shot; "Use but don't waste," he tells them. Lewis would seem to have the same moral affinity with natural forces that made Natty so invincible. Lewis has aim true enough to bring down a bird on the wing with an equally impossible shot; in his case it is a quail at forty yards with an aluminum target arrow (16).

Ed's "grace under pressure" when the time comes that he must hit his target, or die for missing, is surely meant to signify his achievement of the moral secret of "true aim." During his climb up the cliff he undergoes the renewal of his basic instincts and achieves the return of his unconscious to its physical source. The mind-frenzying danger of the epic drama forces him into a position where he has "to make love to the cliff, to fuck it for an extra inch or two in the moonlight" (183). Literally "on the edge between murder and love," he finds that he is so afraid of falling he is "moving," he says, "with the most intimate motions of my body, motions I had never dared use with Martha, or with any other human woman. Fear and a kind of enormous moon-blazing sexuality lifted me" (182). Notice he says "human woman." It is the forces that make the river run with which he is now intimate, more intimate than he has ever dared to be with another repressed human being, far from "his own proper character" yet closer to the pulsing source of sexuality than human partners ever dare approach.

Only once before had he felt nearly as close to these "strong powers" (31-32), and that was when he sensed that the "gold-glowing mote" in the model's eye was alive and seeing him. And when he saw it again during intercourse with Martha he imagined it promised "deliverance" with its suggestion of "other things" beyond the obscuring wall of practical sex (38). Now, on the cliff, so frighteningly close to the nonhuman powers, he longs to see that same gold mote: "I held madly to the human. I looked for a slice of gold like the model's in the river: some freckle, something lovable, in the huge serpent shape of light" (182). There is dramatic irony in this statement, a truth he has yet to learn. The gold mote never did represent the kind of strictly human qualities he seems to ascribe to it. It always was the primal graces of the wilderness, the primitive forces in which human life began and to which it seeks to return, that he was longing for when he fell in love with the gold mote.

The real climax of the story occurs when Ed purifies his body enough to gain the capacity to discover or possibly to create the crevice which saves his life; in ecstasy he declares, "I had both hands in the cliff to the palms, and strength from the stone flowed into me" (172). This may sound like mysticism, but its truth is attested to by such observers of the human being in combat as Robert Graves and Erich Maria Remarque. The sense of self-transcendence, as discussed by Koestler (pp. 31–32), that accompanies the archetypal experience of danger and death and the seemingly supernatural powers acquired by the man suddenly forced to reestablish contact with the earth are described by Paul Bäumer, the hero/narrator of *All Quiet on the Western Front* (1928), in language remarkably similar to Ed's:

From the earth, from the air, sustaining forces pour into us—mostly from the earth. To no man does the earth mean so much as to the soldier. When he presses himself down upon her long and powerfully, when he buries his face and his limbs deep in her from the fear of death by shell-fire, then she is his only friend, his brother, his mother; he stifles his terror and his cries in her silence and her security; she shelters him and gives him a new lease of ten seconds of life, receives him again and often forever.

Earth!—Earth!—Earth!

Earth with thy folds and hollows and holes, into which a man may fling himself and crouch down! In the spasm of terror, under the hailing of annihilation, in the bellowing death of the explosions, O Earth, thou grantest us the great resisting surge of new-won life. Our being, almost utterly carried away by the fury of the storm, streams back through our hands from thee, and we, thy redeemed ones, bury ourselves in thee, and through the long minutes in a mute agony of hope bite into thee with our lips!

At the sound of the first droning of the shells we rush back, in one part of our being, a thousand years. By the animal instinct that is awakened in us we are led and protected. It is not conscious; it is far quicker, much more sure, less fallible, than consciousness. One cannot explain it. A man is walking along without thought or heed;—suddenly he throws himself down on the ground and a storm of fragments flies harmlessly over him;—yet he cannot remember either to have heard the shell coming or to have thought of flinging himself down [Robert Graves had this exact experience, which is recounted in very similar terms to these in *Good-bye to All That* (1929)] . . . we reach the zone where the front begins and become on the instant human animals.

For Ed the purification of the body leads to a purification of the mind, which is demonstrated by his discovery that "the river was running in my mind, and I raised my lids and saw exactly what had been the image of my thought" (176). The secret strength of the hero is now his. His body has brought his mind into touch with nature's ways. His understanding of the human situation is now in balance with the existential reality of natural law. His aspirations are running in harmony with his expectations. His once fear-ridden imagination (pp. 73–74) is vibrating in concert with the way things are. And his nerves steady with the realization that human actions were never intended to matter very much, that there are no eternal cosmic repercussions, only momentary thrashings about. His mood comes to reflect the all-pervasive tone of the universe that he had seen reflected in the river: "It was not that I felt myself turning evil, but that an enormous physical indifference, as vast as the whole abyss of light at my feet, came to me: an indifference not only to the other man's body scrambling and kicking on the ground with an arrow through it, but also to mine" (186).

Northrop Frye's Theory of Modes teaches that the end is literally in the beginning, and so I am led back to my epigraph, the vision of Nebuchadnezzar (Daniel 4:14–16). The message of the Holy One reads:

"Hew down the tree, lop off the branches,
strip away the foliage, scatter the fruit.
　Let the wild beasts flee from its shelter
　　and the birds from its branches,
but leave the stump with its roots in the ground.
　So, tethered with an iron ring,
　let him eat his fill of the lush grass;
　let him be drenched with the dew of heaven
　and share the lot of the beasts in their pasture;
　let his mind cease to be a man's mind,
　and let him be given the mind of a beast."
[New English Bible]

The message of the Holy One is not a curse but a formula for redemption. Daniel informs the king that the tree represents himself and the branches, the society he has built. But amid these human wonders the king has forgotten "that the Most High is sovereign over the kingdom of men and gives it to whom he will." The Lord would have him brought into touch with his animal roots, would have him learn the humility that, as Lewis has discovered, only the life in the wilderness can teach, so that he "may know that from the time you acknowledge the sovereignty of heaven your rule will endure." From Dickey and Remarque we learn a little more of what it means to have to cease thinking human thoughts and "be given the mind of a beast." Nebuchadnezzar did as he was bid and returns with an insight that parallels that which Ed learns in the wilderness: "All dwellers upon earth count for nothing." "At that very time," when he received this insight, according to Nebuchadnezzar, "I returned to my right mind and my majesty and royal splendour were restored to the glory of my kingdom."

Dickey takes his epigraph from another Old Testament prophet, Obadiah: "The pride of thine heart hath deceived thee, thou that dwellest in the clefts of the rock, whose habitation is high; that saith in his heart, Who shall bring me down to the ground?" (Obadiah 3, KJV). Critics have wondered if Dickey meant this as a condemnation of the mountain men or of Ed and Lewis. But Dickey does not mean this as a condemnation at all but as a formula for salvation, the lesson of humility leading the man who learns it to "Mount Zion," infinitely higher than the highest human habitation, where, according to Obadiah, "shall be deliverance" (17, KJV).

Perhaps Dickey's choice of epigraph serves as a warning that Lewis's mystique is not as pure as it should be. "Lewis wanted to be immortal," Ed tells us in the beginning, but by the end, having resisted the pull of the river and having been wounded for it, Lewis learns that "he can die now; he knows that dying is better than immortality" (19, 283). With this knowledge Lewis can return to his society and, like Nebuchadnezzar, live at peace with it. There is no longer any desperate need to "light out for the territory." He can sit by the man-made lake with Ed watching the water skiers, secure in his hard-won feeling for "the true weight and purpose of all water" (283).

Lewis and Ed have learned the indifference to their own lives which is the secret to putting one's body and mind in touch with all life, that is the secret of the hero's power to save lives and to make this salvation the way to a life more abundant. They have learned that deliverance lies *down*river, that a man has only to give himself up to the primal pull of natural forces. So, Ed concludes, "Let the river run" (176).

INDEX

Einstein, Albert, 21, 26, 29, 34-35, 120; Unified Field Theory of, 24, 118-19; see also Relativity
Eliot, T. S., *The Waste Land*, 15
Ellison, Ralph, 5; O'Brien's interview with, 62-63, 100-01; *Invisible Man*, 36-38, 41-42, 98-111, 121; "Richard Wright's Blues " 102-03, 108
Emerson, Ralph Waldo, 71, 76; difference from Melville, 12-13, 15; difference from Poe, 23; transcendental philosophy of, 12, 53, 61, 65-66, 78, 101
ESP, 24, 27, 31
Existentialism, 14, 112-13, 115-16, 121, 126

Faulkner, William, 122; "The Bear," 117
Feidelson, Charles, *Symbolism and American Literature*, 23, 25, 90, 100
Feynman, Richard Phillips, 29
Fiedler, Leslie, *Love and Death in the American Novel*, 62
Firsoff, V. A., 29-30
Fitzgerald, F. Scott, *The Great Gatsby*, 52-53, 63, 131, 133
Forster, E. M., *Aspects of the Novel*, 38
Frazer, Sir James, *The Golden Bough*, 15
Freud, Sigmund, 13, 16, 23, 26, 29, 42, 65, 118; on "castration anxiety," 73-76; on Eros and Thanatos (the life instinct and the death instinct), 67-68, 71-72, 74-75, 80-81, 93-95, 124; on narcissism, 67-69, 70-71, 132; on the "Nirvana principle," 74-75, 93-94; on the "Oedipal project," 39-41; on the "primal horde" theory, 69-70, 78, 106-08; on "repetition compulsion," 37; *Beyond the Pleasure Principle*, 71-73, 94-95; *The Ego and the Id*, 67, 78; *Moses and Monotheism*, 17, 78, 107; *Totem and Taboo*, 107; *Wit and the Unconscious*, 16-17; see also Brown, Norman O. and Marcuse, Herbert
Friedman, Norman, 37
Frye, Northrop, 40; *Anatomy of Criticism*, 35, 46-49, 50-51, 52, 56, 63-64, 108, 128, 134-35, 141; *Fables of Identity*, 35, 36-38, 46, 135

Gamow, George, 96
Gell-Mann, Murray, 30
Goodman, Paul, 10, 32
Graves, Robert, *Good-bye to All That*, 140, 141; *The White Goddess*, 40, 58
Great Chain of Being, 113, 119

Hammett, Dashiell, 135
Hardy, Thomas, 70
Hawthorne, Nathaniel, 13, 62; Melville on, 6-7, 12, 25; *The House of the Seven Gables*, 8; *The Scarlet Letter*, 8-9
Heidegger, Martin, 14
Heisenberg, Werner, the "uncertainty principle" of, 25-26
Hemingway, Ernest, 53, 121, 131, 133; "Big Two-Hearted River," 130; *Men at War*, 73; *For Whom the Bell Tolls*, 51-52, 128
Holman, Harriet R., 23
Homeric Epic, 129-30, 131-32, 135-36
Huxley, Aldous, "The Gioconda Smile," 49-51

I Ching, 24-25

Jameson, Frederic, 9, 11, 19-20, 30, 33
Jeans, Sir James, 24, 26
Jones, Ernest, 93
Jung, Carl, 13, 15, 17, 18, 19, 25; on archetypes, 26-27, 31; on "synchronicity," 27-28, 31; see also Progoff, Ira

Kammerer, Paul, on "seriality," 27
Kesey, Ken, *One Flew Over the Cuckoo's Nest*, 63
Koestler, Arthur, on the "integrative tendency," 81, 94, 96, 117; on the "self-assertive tendency," 81, 87; *The Roots of Coincidence*, 21, 24-32, 40, 124, 140
Levin, Harry, *The Power of Blackness*, 6-7, 89
Levi-Strauss, Claude, "The Structural Study of Myth," 38-39, 44
Lewis, C. S., *The Allegory of Love*, 44; *A Preface to Paradise Lost*, 129-30
London, Jack, 53
Lutwack, Leonard, *Heroic Fiction*, 128-29, 132